Wedding Cakes

I would like to thank my husband Stuart, without whom this book could not have been written, Pauline Giles, my senior teacher at Woodnutt's who executed some of my royal icing designs and whose advice I greatly value, and Diana Beeson, who helped me by piping countless pieces of lace and making many of the small flowers. I also willingly acknowledge the contributions made by my students, who over the years have collectively helped me to clarify so many of the processes and techniques which are a part of contemporary cake decoration. **E.M.**

Published 1988 by Merehurst Press
5 Great James Street
London WC1N 3DA

© Copyright 1988 Merehurst Limited

Co-published in Australia and New Zealand
by Child & Associates, 9 Clearview Place,
Brookvale, Sydney 2100

ISBN 0 948075 82 1

Managing Editor Alison Leach
Editor Jane Struthers
Designer Carole Perks
Photographer Graham Tann, assisted by Yolande Salisbury and Lucy Baker
Typeset by Saxon Graphic Services
Colour Separation by Fotographics Ltd, London–Hong Kong
Printed by Henri Proost, Turnhout, Belgium

The Publishers would like to thank the following for their help:
China supplied by Chinacraft of London, 499 Oxford Street, London W1
and branches
Youngs Franchise Limited, reference Pronuptia, 19-20 Hanover Street,
London W1

Contents

Foreword

It gives me great pleasure to write the foreword for this book. Elaine MacGregor is a well known and highly respected cake decorator. She is a successful writer and teacher, with a school that attracts students from all over the world.

I first met Elaine through my involvement with the British Sugarcraft Guild. Her dedication and determination to achieve the highest possible standards made an instant and lasting impression upon me.

A wedding cake attracts more attention than any other cake and, for this reason, deserves special attention. Elaine MacGregor's book is devoted entirely to wedding cakes and covers many aspects of this fascinating subject. The instructions are comprehensive and easy to follow, with beautiful illustrations.

As far as I am concerned, the main attraction of the book is that it enables the decorator, whatever the standard of artistry, to produce a pleasing, well decorated cake. Novices will find simple, but elegant designs that should not be beyond their capabilities. More experienced students will be able to further their skill, whilst advanced decorators will be delighted with the new and exciting designs to be found in this book.

Wedding Cakes is not a book to be looked at and then placed on the shelf. It is a book to be used and enjoyed — I thoroughly recommend it to you.

Audrey Holding

Introduction

This book is dedicated to all those parents who have experienced the soul-searching moment which occurs just after their devoted daughter has announced her intention of getting married, when she asks winningly, 'You will do the cake, of course, won't you?'

The purpose of this book is to help you overcome the feeling that making occasional birthday cakes and routine Christmas cakes does not provide you with anything like enough experience to enter the stylish and demanding world of wedding confectionery. Even if you have never iced a cake before, in the sections that follow there are a number of cakes that you will be able to make and decorate without great difficulty, and if you feel a little more confident or experienced, you will find others that will extend your skills and give you the greatest satisfaction as you complete the designs. Each of the 25 cakes is identified according to the level of expertise needed to make it.

A most important point to take into consideration when choosing the design for your wedding cake is that the photographs in this book were all taken of the best sides of the most carefully decorated creations from the hands of an experienced cake decorator. If your finished cake isn't quite the way it looks in the book, don't worry too much — you probably haven't had ten years' cake decorating experience! Instead, turn the cake around to show off its best side and bask in the praise and applause that will certainly come your way.

The book is planned so that you can refer to the first few pages whenever you require the basic information common to all cake decoration techniques. Read this entire section before you begin any work, then go over it again after you have decided which cake to make, taking care to note any points that are especially relevant. The main part of the book is arranged by cake shape, decorated to differing levels of skill. Since there is little difference in the keeping qualities of a well-made traditional royal iced cake and one decorated with sugarpaste, there is no technical reason for one style of icing having precedence over the other, and the choice can be on aesthetic grounds alone.

Before you decide which cake to make, remember that there is nothing in the cake decorating rule book that insists on your slavishly following the designs shown here. If the features of two or more cakes appeal to you, why not adapt and combine them to get the result you want? Remember, however, the notion that some cakes are elegant because of their simplicity — a characteristic of good cake design is as much in what is left off as in what is put on! The high point of the ornate style of decoration was the nineteenth century when sugar angels, cherubs and heraldic figures, not to mention columns, flying buttresses, plinths and pillars were almost essential on every cake of quality. Today this style is hardly ever practised, since it demands an excessive amount of time and quite a lot of highly specialised equipment. In recent years, the movement has been towards cakes decorated with natural or sugar flowers, comparatively simple piping work and the use of delicate ribbons to provide colour and to balance the carefully sculpted ornaments placed on the cake.

The celebration of a wedding is one of our most ancient rituals. In all cultures, the events surrounding a betrothal are marked by the presentation of gifts, and by the symbolic practice of giving and receiving tokens to represent purity and fertility. Each aspect of the wedding ritual — the ring, the veil, the feast and the cake — plays its part, and has a counterpart that would have been recognised in ancient Greek, Roman, Egyptian and Chinese wedding ceremonies. In writing this book I felt a great sense of satisfaction in the thought that I was merely continuing to document a cultural tradition that began thousands of years ago. In our increasingly busy lives, we rarely admit to spending a lot of time doing something purely for the love of it, but when it comes to decorating a wedding cake, we are still prepared to put aside any practical considerations for the sake of a beautiful and extravagant design, as others have also done through the ages.

Elaine MacGregor

Cake mixtures

Av. rich fruit cake mix weight	Approx. cooking time	Cake tin (pan) size	No. portions (fruit cake)	No. portions (sponge)
700g (1lb 8oz)	3 hours	round 12.5cm (5in) square 10cm (4in)	8-12	4-5
950g (2lb 2oz)	3¾ hours	round 15cm (6in) square 12.5cm (5in)	15-20	5-8
1.1kg (2lb 8oz)	4 hours	round 17.5cm (7in) square 15cm (6in)	20-25	8-10
1.8kg (4lb)	4½ hours	round 20cm (8in) square 17.5cm (7in)	30-35	10-14
2.8kg (6lb)	5 hours	round 22.5cm (9in) square 20cm (8in)	45-50	14-20
3.6kg (8lb)	5 hours	round 25cm (10in) square 22.5cm (9in)	65-70	20-25
4.5kg (10lb)	5½ hours	round 27.5cm (11in) square 25cm (10in)	80-85	25-30
5.6kg (12lb 8oz)	5½ hours	round 30cm (12in) square 27.5cm (11in)	100-110	30-40
7.2kg (16lb)	6 hours	round 32.5cm (13in) square 30cm (12in)	120-130	40-50
8.5kg (19lb)	7 hours	round 35cm (14in) square 32.5cm (13in)	140-150	50-60

The rich fruit cake recipe is known as an '8oz mix' because it contains that quantity of each of the principal ingredients. To make larger or smaller cakes it is easy to increase or decrease the quantities, but the proportion of ingredients must remain the same, and when the cake is cooking you must remember to adjust the length of the baking time.

You will see, when referring to the chart, that a comparatively small increase in the size of cake tin (pan) requires a fairly significant increase in the amount of rich fruit cake mixture. This is because it is the volume of the tin (the height, length and width) that is important, not just the horizontal area. It is also for this reason that at first glance you appear to do far better when cutting up a 25-cm (10-in) square cake (80-85 portions) than a 20-cm (8-in) square cake (45-50 portions), for example.

To find how many portions you will obtain after allowing a little for wastage, follow the chart to the right-hand column. Use this information at the planning stage, to help you decide whether a single-tier or a multi-tiered cake is required. You will be able to calculate quite accurately the minimum amounts you will need to cater for all your wedding guests and the absent friends who wish to have some cake saved for them.

If you wish to bake an irregularly shaped cake, it is still quite easy to obtain an idea of the approximate weight of cake mixture you need, and therefore the number of portions you will have. Simply fill the tin with water to the depth you would expect to fill it with cake mixture, then weigh it. Subtract the weight of the tin itself and you are left with the approximate weight of the mixture you will need. You don't have to be too accurate, and you can round the result up or down, to give you a weight from which the recipe quantities can be calculated.

Any small omissions or substitutions of ingredients that you make to suit your own taste won't ruin the results, but it is very important follow the method and sequence of mixing and baking the cake.

Rich fruit cake

225g (8oz) sultanas
225g (8oz) currants
225g (8oz) raisins
125g (4oz) glacé cherries, halved
50g (2oz) mixed peel (optional)
50g (2oz) almonds, unblanched and
    chopped
225g (8oz) butter
225g (8oz) dark brown molasses
    sugar
4 eggs, slightly beaten
225g (8oz) plain (all-purpose) flour
50g (2oz) self-raising flour
5ml (1 tsp) mixed spice
5ml (1 tsp) cinnamon
1ml (¼ tsp) nutmeg
1ml (¼ tsp) salt
choose one of the following:
150ml (¼ pint) sherry
150ml (¼ pint) brandy
150ml (¼ pint) orange juice
75ml (⅛ pint) each sherry and
    orange juice

Soak all the dried fruits and almonds in the alcohol or orange juice the night before. Set the oven at 220°C (425°F) Gas Mark 7 when you start to mix the cake. Beat together the butter and sugar, then add a little of the eggs at a time. Sift together the dry ingredients, then stir them into the creamed butter mixture, alternating them with the dried fruits and their liquid. Turn into a well-greased 20-cm (8-in) square or 22.5-cm (9-in) round cake tin (pan), reduce the temperature of the oven to 140°C (275°F) Gas Mark 2 and place the cake in the centre of an electric oven, and on the bottom shelf of a gas oven for approximately 3 hours or until cooked.

Light fruit cake

225g (8oz) mixed dried fruit
75ml (⅛ pint) orange juice or sherry
225g (8oz) butter
225g (8oz) caster (superfine) sugar
3 eggs, lightly beaten
225g (8oz) plain (all-purpose) flour

Soak the dried fruit in the orange juice or sherry overnight. Set the oven at 170°C (350°F) Gas Mark 3-4. Cream together the butter and sugar, then add the eggs. If they separate, stir in a little flour before adding more egg mixture. Stir in the fruit, then fold in the flour. Turn into a well greased 20-cm (8-in) round cake tin (pan) and bake for 2½ hours or until cooked.

Madeira cake

175g (6oz) unsalted butter
175g (6oz) caster (superfine) sugar
2 eggs, lightly beaten
175g (6oz) self-raising flour
75g (3oz) plain (all-purpose) flour
15ml (1 tsp) lemon juice

Set the oven at 170°C (350°F) Gas Mark 3-4. Cream together the fat and the sugar, then add the eggs, a little at a time. If they start to curdle, beat in a little flour before adding more of the egg mixture. Sift the flours together, then fold into the creamed mixture. When all the flour has been incorporated the mixture should have the consistency of lightly whipped cream. Add the lemon juice, then turn into a greased and lined 17.5-cm (7-in) square cake tin (pan), smooth the top and bake for 1 hour, or until golden brown and springy to the touch. Leave in the tin to cool before turning out the cake.

Degree of skill

Each cake has been given a symbol to denote the degree of skill required to decorate it.

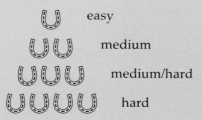

    easy

    medium

    medium/hard

    hard

Important: use only one set of measurements. The quantities given in metric are not always exact conversions of the imperial measurements. Cup conversions of imperial measurements are given below.

Imperial	Cups
¼ pint liquid	⅔ cup
½ pint liquid	1¼ cups
1 pint liquid	2½ cups
2 pints liquid	5 cups
1lb granulated or caster (superfine) sugar	2 cups
1lb brown sugar	2 cups
1lb icing (confectioner's) sugar	3½ cups
1lb butter	2 cups
1lb flour	4 cups
1lb dried fruit	3 cups
8oz glacé cherries	1 cup
4oz chopped nuts	1 cup
1oz flour	¼ cup
1oz granulated or caster (superfine) sugar	2 tablespoons
1oz butter	2 tablespoons

Cake pillars

Three, four or even five tiers of wedding cake, elegantly set up and sitting in the spotlight of everyone's attention and admiration, can strike fear into the heart of every head waiter or hostess. They've all heard the story about the wedding cake that fell down. However, there is no need for concern as there are several fail-safe techniques for preventing such an accident happening to you.

Pillars for royal iced cakes

In general, plaster cake pillars are used with royal iced cakes. For a three-tier cake, it is usual to support the middle tier on 8.75-cm (3½-in) or 10-cm (4-in) high pillars, and support the top tier on pillars that are 12-mm (½-in) shorter to maintain the proportions of the cake. If the royal icing has been correctly made and applied, it will provide a finish that is sufficiently strong to support the weight of the two upper tiers of a three-tier cake. However, if there is any doubt about the strength of the icing, or a cake of four or more tiers is to be assembled, it is prudent to place a thin cake card on the icing of the bottom tier so as to spread the load across its surface.

As an alternative to using groups of three or four plaster cake pillars, you can buy small stands that consist of a pair of square or circular clear plastic plates separated by four equal lengths of rod or tubing. These sets, known as separators, are placed between the cakes and replace the conventional pillars, thus eliminating any concern about the cakes collapsing should the supports sink through the icing.

Pillars for sugarpaste cakes

The increasingly popular method of covering cakes with sugarpaste has led to another method of ensuring the stability of tiered cakes. Here, hollow plastic pillars are used, but they are only for decorative purposes. The cakes are really supported by wooden skewers which pass through the centre of the pillars and right through the cake, to rest on the cake board. One advantage of this technique is that any unevenness in the surface of a lower tier does not affect the stability of those above it since, provided the supporting pillars are of equal length, they will automatically support the higher tiers horizontally.

To set up a cake with hollow pillars, rest them in position on the surface of the icing, then place a straight edge or ruler on top of them. Hold a skewer vertically beside the cake, with its tip resting on the cake board, then mark the skewer to show the depth of the cake itself combined with the height of the pillar and the thickness of the ruler. Cut the required number of skewers to exactly the requisite length, then push them into the icing and through the cake. Take care to ensure that you push each skewer down vertically, as they must provide a completely horizontal support for the next tier. Lower a pillar over each skewer, and you will have a strong and stable support. Check to ensure that the tops of the skewers are aligned to each other with a spirit level. When the cake is assembled, there should be a little play in each pillar, since it is not intended to bear any of the weight of the cake it is supporting.

Positioning cake pillars

If a pillar is placed incorrectly, it can spoil the appearance of a tiered cake as well as jeopardise its stability. The diagram shows how to work out the positioning of the pillars on various shaped cakes, each time following the same principles (see page 80).

Trace around the largest cake tin (pan) on to a sheet of tracing paper, then cut around it to make a template. Mark the template at the points where the pillars are to be placed. Four pillars are most commonly used for square or octagonal cakes, and three are used for most other shapes.

The chart shows the positioning of three or four pillars on all the popular shapes and sizes. The captions suggest how to make specific templates for square, petal, heart-shaped, round, hexagonal and oval cakes.

Patterns and Sizing

Some of the templates in this book will have to be sized before they can be used in a cake design.

If the pattern is exactly the right size, you need only transfer it to the iced surface of the cake by scratching around the outlines with a scriber. Do not use a pencil, or you will deposit small amounts of graphite on the icing.

If the design is not the right size, it must be enlarged or reduced. To overcome any difficulties this may cause, the patterns have been laid on a 2.5-cm (1-in) grid. Transfer on to tracing paper and place it over the chosen design. With a sharp pencil, trace over the outline and any other important features. Now draw another grid, with the same number of squares, but this time make it the same size as the area of cake on which the design will be iced. Reproduce the outlines on the new grid, working square by square to help you maintain the correct proportions.

You can use the same technique when creating patterns in brush embroidery or straightforward piping, for the sides of a tiered wedding cake. Measure the circumference and depth of each cake, then cut out a strip of paper to these dimensions. Fold each strip into halves, quarters and eighths, both lengthways and crossways, to form a pattern of rectangular folds. Using these as a grid pattern, transfer the original design on to the strip of paper, using the rectangles as guides. With a little care, this will be accurately proportioned and of exactly the right overall dimensions to fit each of the cakes.

Icings and marzipan

Royal icing

white of 1 medium egg
350g (12oz) icing (confectioner's)
  sugar, sifted
lemon juice

Place the egg white in a large clean and completely greasefree bowl and break it up, using a palette knife. Very gradually add the sifted icing (confectioner's) sugar, 15ml (1 tbsp) at a time, beating very thoroughly with the knife. If the icing is not beaten sufficiently, the finished icing will have a dull, grainy texture. Add a few drops of lemon juice to whiten it and improve its strength. When the icing is ready it should be stiff enough to stand up in peaks and should have a smooth, creamy appearance. If it is too stiff, you can dilute it with a few drops of water, and if too runny you can thicken it with more icing sugar.

Sugarpaste

25g (1oz) powdered gelatine
300ml (10 fl oz) water
450g (1lb) granulated sugar
125g (4oz) liquid glucose
25g (1oz) glycerine
5ml (1 level tsp) cream of tartar
125g (4oz) white vegetable fat
1.4kg (3lb) icing (confectioner's)
  sugar, sifted

Place the gelatine in a bowl with half the water, then stand in a saucepan of hot water and allow to dissolve slowly and thoroughly. Place the granulated sugar, glucose, glycerine, cream of tartar and the remaining water in a wide heavy-based saucepan and stir over medium heat until every grain of sugar has dissolved, then bring to the boil, ensuring that no sugar crystals adhere to the sides of the saucepan. Boil rapidly until the mixture reaches the soft ball stage — 110°-115°C (230°-240°F) on a sugar thermometer. Remove from the heat and immediately place the saucepan in a bowl of cold water. Allow to cool for 3-4 minutes, then stir in the vegetable fat and dissolved gelatine. Slowly stir in the icing (confectioner's) sugar, adding a little at a time, until the mixture has formed a smooth paste. Leave in an air-tight container for 24 hours before use. If necessary, knead in extra icing sugar to obtain the required consistency. This quantity should be sufficient to cover an average-sized three-tier wedding cake, or a large two-tier cake.

Pastillage

10ml (2 tsp) powdered gelatine
25ml (5 tsp) cold water
450g (1lb) icing (confectioner's)
  sugar, sifted
15ml (3 tsp) gum tragacanth
10ml (2 tsp) liquid glucose
10ml (2 tsp) white vegetable fat
1 egg white, medium

Soak the gelatine in the cold water for 30 minutes. Place the sugar and gum tragacanth in a mixing bowl and heat over a saucepan of hot water. Add the liquid glucose and vegetable fat to the bowl of gelatine, then hold over a pan of hot water and heat until they dissolve. Once the sugar is warm to the touch, warm the blades of an electric beater, then slowly begin to beat the mixture. Add the liquids and the egg white. Turn the beater up to maximum speed and beat for about 15 minutes. The longer and harder the mixture is beaten, the whiter it will be.

Petal paste

150g (5oz) petal paste powder
15ml (3tsp) water

This unique instant flower paste powder is available through specialised cake decorators. It is a mixture of sugar and edible gums, and the addition of a little water will turn it into pastillage. Place 15ml (3 tsp) of water in a small bowl and sift seven-eighths of the petal paste powder container into the water, stirring well until all the powder is incorporated. Leave the bowl covered for 5 minutes. Sift the remaining powder on to a clean working surface and knead the pre-mixed paste until the entire mixture is smooth and elastic. For more plasticity, add a pea-sized ball of white vegetable fat to the paste and knead well. Store the paste in an air-tight container. Although it can be used as soon as it is made, for best results, it should be stored for 24 hours before use.

Marzipan

450g (1lb) granulated sugar
150ml (¼ pint) plus 60ml (4 tbsp)
  water
large pinch cream of tartar
350g (12oz) ground almonds
2 egg whites
icing (confectioner's) sugar
almond essence (optional)

Place the sugar and water in a large saucepan and heat very gently, stirring with a metal spoon. Do not allow the syrup to boil until every grain of sugar has dissolved. Add the cream of tartar and bring the syrup to the boil, then boil rapidly without stirring until it reaches the soft ball stage—110°-115°C (230°-240°F) on a sugar thermometer. Do not overboil, or the icing will thicken and be crumbly to handle. To test for soft ball, drop a small teaspoonful of the syrup into a cup of cold water—it should form a soft ball when rubbed between the fingers. Stop the syrup boiling by placing the base of the saucepan in cold water, then immediately stir in the ground almonds and unbeaten egg whites. Return the pan to a low heat and stir until the mixture thickens slightly. Turn the mixture out on to a marble slab, a plastic laminated surface or a wooden board, and work it until it cools and thickens. When it is cold enough, knead the mixture with your hands until it is smooth, using a light dusting of sifted icing (confectioner's) sugar. It will take up to half its weight in icing sugar, but if a lot of sugar is kneaded in, you must add some almond essence to the mixture as well. Store in an air-tight jar or thick polythene bag until the marzipan is ready to use. If it dries out, it can be moistened with a little egg white. This recipe makes 900g (2lb) marzipan, but it can be doubled in quantity. If you want to increase the quantities still further, you must use a very large saucepan and work surface.

Covering cakes

Working with royal icing

You should apply at least three coats of royal icing to a cake to obtain a perfect finish, so always make up a sufficient quantity for all coats at one time. A 25-cm (10-in) cake needs a batch of icing made with 450g (1lb) icing (confectioner's) sugar, and an average three-tier cake a batch made with approximately 1.4kg (3lb) of icing sugar.

Put the egg whites into a clean, greasefree bowl, and lightly stir them before leaving them overnight. This allows some of the water in the albumen to evaporate. Make up the royal icing and use it immediately to apply the first coating to the cake. When you are not working with the royal icing, cover the bowl with a clean damp tea towel, then cover that with a piece of plastic wrap. Put the cake to one side for 24 hours to allow the foundation coat of icing to dry. Stir the remaining icing gently, being careful not to introduce too much air into the mixture, and apply the second coat. Set aside for a further 24 hours, then repeat the process to obtain the final, smooth finish. Leaving the icing for a total period of 48 hours (or even longer if you wish) allows the chemical and physical structure of the icing to change from a light, highly aerated, meringue-like mixture into one with a heavier, creamier and smoother texture.

Place the cake on a turntable and put 45ml (3 tbsp) of icing on the centre of the cake with a palette knife. With a paddling movement, spread the icing towards the sides of the cake with a wide-bladed 20-cm (8-in) or 25-cm (10-in) palette knife. If you see any air bubbles, use a rocking motion of the blade across the icing to eliminate them. Slowly turn the cake while holding the knife steady with its blade almost flat, and just resting on the icing. As the cake moves under the blade, the icing will be dispersed evenly over its surface. If necessary, draw the icing out from the centre to cover the edges of the cake top.

Hold a steel or plastic straight edge, which must be longer than the width or diameter of the cake, firmly at each end, then tilt it at a shallow angle to the surface of the cake and draw it steadily across the icing towards you. Then pivot the straight edge, so that its other long edge is in contact with the icing, and push it gently back in the opposite direction. If you end up with icing on both sides of the straight edge, you are turning it rather than pivoting or rocking it. After one complete sweep in each direction, the icing may not be completely flat, so if necessary repeat this double action. If, after several attempts, you are not satisfied with the finish, remove as much icing as possible, beat the mixture and begin again. The first coating is primarily to seal the cake, so it does not have to look perfect. The second coat will hide any serious imperfections, and give you a proper foundation for the finishing coat. Leave to dry before continuing.

When coating the sides of the cake, use a rigid plastic or stainless steel scraper to remove the excess icing and smooth the remaining mixture. To cover the sides, take some icing on the blade of the palette knife and transfer it to the cake as you rotate the turntable, using a paddling motion to remove any air bubbles. Repeat the process until there is a layer of icing completely covering the sides. Next, hold the edge of the scraper against the cake in roughly the 2 o'clock position, grasp the board with your other hand at the 12 o'clock position, and slowly rotate the cake in an anticlockwise direction, holding the scraper still. As the icing builds up against the scraper, return it to the bowl of unused icing. Now rotate the turntable once more, this time tidying up the edge between the side and upper surfaces by scraping the excess icing from the join between the sides and top. If you are working on the sides of any cake, other than a round one, you will probably find it much easier if you hold the cake stationary on the turntable and, keeping your 'icing arm' in a relaxed but fixed position, use a rocking movement in the upper part of your body to smooth the icing over the cake's sides. Clean up the cake board between coatings, as the side scraper will catch against any dried icing as you apply subsequent layers.

Working with sugarpaste

Many of the cakes illustrated in this book are covered with sugarpaste, also known as rolled fondant. Its main advantage over royal icing is that it can be used to cover a cake in a single operation.

If you intend to colour the sugarpaste, first calculate how much paste you will need for the entire cake, then colour the whole batch and divide it into portions. In this way, you will ensure that all the sugarpaste is of the same shade. When working colour through the paste, or rolling it out, only sprinkle enough icing (confectioner's) sugar on your work surface to prevent the paste from sticking. Using too much sugar will make the paste dry out, so that it cracks after being applied to the cake. If the paste does become too dry, add one or two drops of glycerine and knead

---

Making sugar flowers

Plunger or blossom cutters are used to make most of the smaller flowers; each one is then threaded over an artificial stamen and fixed in place with a minute quantity of royal icing. To attach five or six of these flowers to a piece of floristry wire, bind them to the wire with a small strip of green or white plastic floristry tape. Larger, individual flowers, such as carnations, daisies and sweet peas, are usually made from shaped pastillage petals assembled over a single length of wire. Flowers with long stems, such as fuchsias and some lilies, are assembled around the stamens themselves, which in turn are wired to a stronger stem with plastic tape. To make a posy, bind together a large quantity of flowers on short stems with plastic tape. For very large sprays, an additional binding of strong floristry wire, similar to fuse wire, is used.

well. Never roll the paste out on cornflour (cornstarch), as it could cause fermentation between the marzipan and sugarpaste.

When colouring sugarpaste, use specially made concentrated food colours, not the highly diluted liquids found in most super-markets. Dip a skewer or cocktail stick (wooden toothpick) into the colour, then draw it across the paste, wiping the colour from the skewer. Then knead the paste as though it were dough, to distribute the colour, adding more if required. Check that the colour is evenly distributed by cutting the paste in two with a clean knife. If it is full of deeper coloured swirls, continue to knead it, then test again until the cut section is of an even colour.

The sugarpaste can now be rolled out, or divided into the correct proportions required for each section if you are making a tiered cake. Remember to keep the portions you are not using well wrapped up and as air-tight as possible. Roll out the paste on a dusting of icing sugar, turning it half a turn at intervals while rolling it out until it is large enough to cover the sides and top of the cake. Now paint the pre-viously marzipanned cake with alcohol, to make a good bond for the sugarpaste. Using alcohol helps to sterilise the surface and im-proves the flavour. Rum, brandy or sherry are normally used, but you can use isopropyl alcohol which is available in small quantities from a chemist's shop (pharmacy).

Moisten the marzipanned sur-face, then pick up the paste, sup-porting it over the palms of your hand and your forearms. Place it over the cake, with the edge of the paste overlapping the far side of the cake. Carefully slide one hand out from under the icing and gently firm the paste against the back of the cake. Slowly withdraw the other hand, taking care not to stretch or tear a hole in the paste, and smooth it against the top of the cake. Make sure you do not trap any air under the surface. If the cake has corners, flare the paste and mould it against the corners first, using the soft part of your palm to stroke the icing into place. Next, smooth the icing against the sides, and trim off any excess around the base with a palette knife. You can create a really even

and glossy surface by polishing the icing with a large plastic smoother. Use a smaller one, or a special cake smoother with a bevelled edge, to flatten the sides and tidy up the top edges and corners.

If there is an air pocket or bubble under the paste, prick it with a pin, held at an angle, force out the air, then smooth the icing again. Use a pin with a large coloured head, as this is easy to see — if you can't find the pin you used when you are cleaning up later on, there is always the danger that it has been rolled into the paste.

The easiest way to secure a cake to its board is to place a small cone of moistened sugarpaste in the cen-tre of the board. Pick up the cake by sliding it off the edge of the work surface on to the palm of your hand, and hold it over the board. Quickly withdraw your hand, allowing the cake to fall on to the board and, using the smoother, press down the cake to flatten it against the sugarpaste cone, ensur-ing you do not leave any finger-prints.

If you intend to decorate, using embossing tools or crimpers, you must do so while the sugarpaste is still soft, and within 30 minutes of covering the cake.

Working with marzipan

To achieve a good coating of icing on a cake, you must give it a proper foundation, by applying a smooth, even layer of marzipan.

If the cake did not rise in the centre during baking, pack the hollow area with marzipan before turning the cake over. This way, the surface from the bottom of the tin (pan) becomes the top of the cake, and should be very even. Conversely, if the cake has risen too much, shave off a slice with a very sharp knife so that it becomes flat, then roll a thin sausage of marzipan and flatten it against the top edges of the cake so that, when turned upside down, a good seal is formed at the perimeter with the cake board. Use a palette knife to mould it on to the cake and apply a little boiled sieved apricot jam or fresh egg white to stick the two together. Ensure that the sides of the cake are smooth by filling any small holes in the surface.

When using royal icing Roll out a strip of marzipan for the sides of the cake, and cut it to the correct height and length. Round cakes require a strip about three times the width of the cake, but square ones need four separate sections, each the length of one side. Turn the marzipan over so that the smoother side is face down, and brush the exposed surface with the hot jam or egg white. When working with a round cake, lift it on to its edge and roll it along the strip, picking up the marzipan as you roll. Firm it into place using a flexible plastic smoother. Then trim the edges and joins carefully. Apply the four sec-tions individually for a square cake and make sure that the joins at the corners are neat and properly sea-led, if necessary sticking them with a little extra jam or egg white. Now roll out the marzipan for the top of the cake to a thickness of about 6mm ($\frac{1}{4}$in) and turn it over. Brush hot jam or egg white over an area the size of the cake top, using the cake tin as a guide and adding an extra 12mm ($\frac{1}{2}$in) to allow for the marzipan at the sides. Place the cake on the marzipan and press it gently to fix the two together, then cut off any excess. Turn the cake the right way up and trim any rough edges, ensuring that the top joins the sides properly. Use a flexible plastic smoother to lightly polish the marzipanned surfaces and remove any finger-prints or irregularities. If possible, allow the marzipan to harden for at least 48 hours in a dry atmosphere.

When using sugarpaste Roll out the marzipan until it is large enough to drape over the top and sides of the cake. First form the marzipan on to any corners. Flare it out slightly over the first corner to unfold any pleats and, using the palm of your hand only, ease it on to the corner with an upward movement. Repeat this process on the other corners, then ease the marzipan tightly against the sides of the cake and smooth the top in the same way. Then proceed as above.

Spring garlands

Ingredients
25-cm (10-in) round fruit cake
boiled sieved apricot jam or egg white
1.4kg (3lb) marzipan
water or alcohol
900g (2lb) royal icing
125g (4oz) royal icing for piping
moss green food colouring

Equipment
32.5-cm (13-in) round cake board
silver banding
No1 nozzle
No5 nozzle
vegetable parchment piping bags
tracing paper
scriber
1 metre (1⅛ yards) peach tear ribbon
5cm (2in) white lantern ribbon
3 small silk tea rose buds
2 medium white silk roses
2 sprays of peach silk jasmine
4 medium peach silk marigolds
8 lengths dangling silk lily of the valley, cut to
   make 48 flowers
white opaque candle vase

Number of portions
55-65

Amount of work involved
Approximately 2½ hours

This cake shows the classic elegance of a royal iced cake, and even the most inexperienced decorator will be able to create this attractive design. Remember to allow at least three days to complete the work, since you must leave time to apply an even layer of marzipan and also to apply a minimum of three coats of royal icing, allowing each coating to dry for 24 hours before applying the next. Apply a thin coat of royal icing to the cake board and leave to dry. Icing the board not only helps to seal the cake to the board, thus helping to prolong its freshness, but also reflects light up on to the sides of the cake to give it a softer, more delicate appearance. Trim the edges of the board with silver banding, securing the join with a little royal icing.

When all the icing is dry, place the cake in the centre of the iced cake board. Using a No5 nozzle and white royal icing of a piping consistency, pipe a shell border around the base of the cake, and another around the top edge. These borders are very quick to ice and have the advantage of hiding any imperfections that might otherwise be visible on the edges of the cake.

The simple flower rosettes are repeated six times around the sides of the cake. You can either use silk flowers or make your own flowers from thinly rolled pastillage or petal paste *(see below)*. Make a circular template of the required size on a sheet of tracing paper, then place it on the iced side of the cake and scribe around the outline.

To make the small icing leaves, use moss green-coloured royal icing and a No1 nozzle, piping teardrop shapes between each flower and directly on to the iced surface of the cake. Arrange a selection of ribbon loops and curls, and the silk flowers in the glass vase and place it in the centre of the cake, allowing some of the flowers and ribbon curls to trail over the edge of the vase on to the cake.

Using blossom plunger cutters
Roll out a piece of pastillage or petal paste into a very thin sheet, then cut out a flower shape with a blossom plunger cutter and press against a piece of foam rubber which has been lightly dusted with cornflour (cornstarch), allowing the foam to cup the paste into a flower shape. This is the basis of almost all flower-making from sugar.

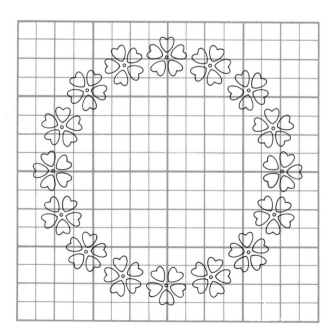

Autumn gold

Ingredients
17.5-cm (7-in) round fruit cake
25-cm (10-in) round fruit cake
boiled sieved apricot jam or egg white
1.7kg (3lb 10oz) marzipan
water or alcohol
2.1kg (4lb 12oz) sugarpaste
450g (1lb) royal icing for piping
10ml (2 tsp) piping gel
apple green food colouring
chestnut food colouring
Christmas red food colouring
Cornish cream food colouring
dark brown food coluring
moss green food colouring
peach food colouring
skintone food colouring

Equipment
15-cm (6-in) round gold-coloured cake board,
   12-mm (½-in) thick
22.5-cm (9-in) round gold-coloured cake board,
   12-mm (½-in) thick
35-cm (14-in) round gold-coloured cake board,
   12-mm (½-in) thick
scriber
No0 nozzle
No1 nozzle
No5 nozzle
vegetable parchment piping bags
No3 sable paintbrush
2.5 metres (2½ yards) 3-mm (⅛-in) russet
   satin ribbon
4 sugar rose hips
4 sugar rose leaves
5 sugar ivy leaves
5 sugar acorns
8 sugar oak leaves
5 sugar maple leaves
set of 3 rose leaf cutters
set of 3 ivy leaf cutters

Number of portions
80-90

Amount of work involved
Approximately 6½ hours

As well as the traditional white or pink wedding cakes, you can plan some very effective and unusual colour schemes, perhaps taking your inspiration from the season in which the wedding will take place. Here, russets, muted oranges and greens have been used to create the perfect cake for an autumn wedding.

Cover the cakes with marzipan and chestnut-coloured sugarpaste in the usual way and leave to dry, then position the cakes on the two largest boards. The smallest board is placed beneath the upper tier when the cake is assembled, to separate the two cakes without using a cake stand or cake pillars.

Brush embroidery, also known as guipure lace-work as it creates an effect similar to the heavily embroidered lace of the same name, is a technique in which designs are piped on to a cake and then textured with a soft damp paintbrush. Using white icing on a white background gives a very delicate effect, but contrasting colours can look very striking and interesting.

The technique is really little more than painting with very smooth and creamy royal icing. To achieve the right consistency, add a very small quantity of piping gel to a batch of royal icing made the day before, working to a ratio of 2.5ml (½ tsp) of gel to a cup of icing. This will decrease the rate at which the mixture dries and allow more time for the brushwork necessary to smooth the icing into flowing lines and patterns.

Having scribed the design of your choice on to the cake with a template, pipe around an outline with a No1 nozzle. If you use a smaller nozzle you will not have enough icing to brush, and using a bigger one will give you too much icing, unless your design is very large. Apply a second line of icing very close to the first, or at intervals around the inside edge of the outline. Begin work immediately, using a No3 paintbrush that has been slightly dampened with water and then squeezed between your fingers to flatten the brush hairs and give them a slight curl or curve. Stroke the still fluid icing from the outside towards the centre or base of the design, using the curved side of the brush and not just its tip. Good brushwork consists of regular, gentle strokes which result in a smooth, even finish. You will achieve a more realistic result on leaves and petals if the direction of your brushstrokes follows the general direction of their veins and other natural contours. The veins may be piped on while the brushwork is still wet, in which case they will blend into the background icing or, for a raised effect, they can be piped on with a No0 or No1 nozzle when the brushed icing is dry.

When completed, the entire surface of the object painted will have a thin coating of icing. Graduating the thickness of the icing so that it is

raised either at the outline or the centre will give a more realistic effect. For even greater contrast, a second heavy line of icing can be piped on to the foreground of the design when it has dried. This must then be carefully brushed out at the edges to form a continuous smooth join with the rest of the pattern. This technique is especially useful for creating the curled edges of rose petals or the teardrop-shaped tips of chrysanthemum petals.

When using colour in a design, prepare a small piping bag of each of the colours and complete the work section by section. If working on the Autumn Gold cake, work on one leaf at a time alternating between the colours and piping wet on wet, blending them together with the paintbrush to form a smooth graduation between the colours. The painting in of fine detail such as highlights requires as little moisture as possible. Alternatively, dry petal dust can be brushed on to the design to enhance the effect and deepen the colour.

Complete the cakes by piping a line of shells around the base of each cake, using chestnut-coloured royal icing and a No5 nozzle. Then pipe a dot of dark brown royal icing, using a No0 nozzle, between each shell and leave to dry. Trim each cake with narrow satin ribbon, securing the join with royal icing and then hiding it with a neat bow. Assemble the two tiers, then decorate the top tier with the sugar rose hips and leaves which have been wired into a spray.

Cake decorators' colours
Cake decorators' colours are very concentrated, so keep adding very small amounts to the icing until you have achieved the required shade. However, because they are made from a limited range of both natural and artificial ingredients, these colours are not as light-fast as conventional dyes and pigments (which are not suitable for use in the food industry), so expect colours to fade slightly in strong sunlight, especially blues and purples.

Edwardian extravaganza

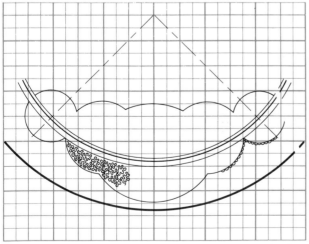

This pattern is for the piping on the board (convex side of the curve) and top of cake (concave side of curve)
The heavy outside curve represents the cake board

Sugar cupids, cherubs, heraldic creatures or classical sculptures — in Edwardian times, these were all major sources of inspiration to anyone wishing to prove themselves as master confectioners. The spirit of this heavily embellished style of decoration lives on today, as in this cake.

Before embarking on this cake, you must have some experience of piping techniques, though you should find it quite easy as long as you don't work in too much of a hurry. To make the project simpler, you can buy the curved sugar leaves from a cake decoration shop. Alternatively, you can make your own *(see page 18)*.

Cover each cake with marzipan and royal icing in the usual way, then leave to dry. Cover each board with a thin layer of royal icing, position the cakes in the centre of the boards and leave to dry. Then decorate the edges with silver banding. To make the grapes, make a template and scribe the outlines on to the cakes so that each cake has four patterns of grapes. Using a No1 nozzle and white royal icing, pipe the stems, then pipe a teardrop-shaped shell down the side of each cake with a No9 nozzle, with the widest part of the shell uppermost. This is to be the filling beneath the grapes themselves. Using a No3 nozzle, pipe the lowest grape in the cluster just below the pointed end of the shell, and then two more on top of it immediately above the first grape, so that all three grapes just touch each other. Pipe three more in the third row, four in the fourth row and five in the fifth row. The sixth and top row has only three grapes, which are piped just on to the top edge of the shell, now completely covered with the cluster of grapes. Next, using a No68 leaf nozzle or a piping bag with its end cut in a V-shape, first pipe two or three leaves and then pipe a final single grape at the very top of the cluster, so that it hides the stem of the leaves. Repeat the process for each bunch of grapes, reducing the size of the clusters on the top tier by using a No2 nozzle, if you wish. Leave to dry.

Next, pipe the linework on to the cakes and coated cake boards, using the templates provided, scribe the outlines on to the cakes and pipe the foundation line with a No3 nozzle, then carefully pipe directly over it with a No2 nozzle. If you wish, you can overpipe once or twice more, using a smaller nozzle each time and piping the uppermost line with a No0 or No00 nozzle. You can add further embellishments by repeating the overpiping at a distance of about 6mm (¼in) to create a tramline effect, thus doubling the density of the piping and placing more emphasis on the linework of the pattern. Finish the base of this linework with a small scalloped line piped with a No0 nozzle.

Now pipe carefully spaced continuous patterns of meandering curves, known as cornelli work, inside the linework, using a No0 nozzle. Do not let the trail of icing double over itself or let the continuous series of loops break. Pipe a line of heavy beading, with a No3 nozzle, around the top and bottom edges of each cake, then pipe a single diagonal line across each bead with a No1 nozzle. With a No2 nozzle, pipe a teardrop of icing below

each bead. In this style of decorating, the larger sizes of nozzles are invariably used because it is the very boldness of the decoration that gives the cake its character.

To fix the curved leaves to the cakes, place a small dab of royal icing on the top and bottom of each leaf and then place gently in position. Assemble the cakes, then decorate the top tier with an arrangement of silk flowers and leaves on the remaining cake pillar, and a plaster cupid. Place the other cupid on the lower tier.

Making curved sugar leaves or 'off pieces'

Adding a pinch of gum tragacanth to the royal icing will make it less brittle and strengthen the finished leaves. Copy the leaf template provided on to a sheet of thin tracing paper and place it under a sheet of waxed paper slightly larger than the template. Over this place a piece of white tulle cut in the shape of the template and stick it to the waxed paper with a dot of royal icing. Using a No2 nozzle, pipe the outlines and the centre line on to the tulle, then the leaves and clusters of grapes or flowers, ensuring that the piped lines touch each other wherever indicated by the design. Work as quickly as possible so that the icing does not have time to dry. When you have finished piping, transfer the leaf, with its waxed paper backing, to a 30 x 20-cm (12 x 8-in) plastic corrugated sheet, with parallel ridges set about 5cm (2in) apart, so that each leaf begins with a concave curve and ends with a convex curve. Repeat the process for each leaf, then allow them to dry overnight in this position. Carefully separate them from their waxed paper backing and fix them to the cake.

The large leaf is optional — a similar design is available commercially

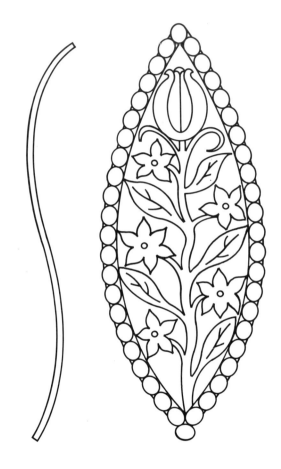

Marriage lines

Ingredients
25-cm (10-in) square fruit cake
boiled sieved apricot jam or egg white
1.5kg (3lb 4oz) marzipan
water or alcohol
1.1kg (2lb 8oz) royal icing
175g (6oz) royal icing for piping
300g (10oz) silver dragées

Equipment
35-cm (14-in) square cake board
tracing paper
scriber
soft sponge or palette knife
No1 nozzle
No2 nozzle
No3 nozzle
vegetable parchment piping bags
pair of tweezers
paintbrush
silver banding
4 double silver plastic wedding rings
4 silver plastic slippers

Number of portions
80-85

Amount of work involved
Approximately 2½ hours

The most distinctive feature of this very simple cake is the contrast in texture between the smooth royal icing of the central areas and the lightly roughened surfaces at the corners. This icing is not intended to look as irregular as of a typical snow scene, but is meant to look stippled.

Cover the cake with marzipan and royal icing in the usual way. Position the cake on the board. Apply a thin layer of royal icing to the cake board and leave to dry. Copy the template provided and use it to mark the position for the overpiped lines at each corner. Ensure that each corner is identical, then mark out the central decoration of the bow and two rings using the template. Place about 15ml (1 tbsp) of royal icing in a saucer, then dab a soft sponge into the icing and pat it gently against the cake. Practise this first, if you wish, bearing in mind that the more icing you use, the rougher the finish will be. Carefully apply the stippled icing to the four corners of the cake, working right up to the lines marking the edge of the pattern on both the sides and the top. For a heavier, rougher effect, apply the icing directly on to the cake with a palette knife, then use the flat of the blade to pull the icing up into sharp peaks. Leave to dry.

Pipe the outline of the centre bow with a No1 nozzle, then flood each section with royal icing (see page 27). Pipe tiny dots around the outer edges of the bow. Using a No3 nozzle, pipe the rings in one continuous circle and, while the icing is still soft, decorate them with silver dragées, positioned with tweezers. Now pipe the lower line around the stippled area on the top and sides of the cake with a No3 nozzle and leave to dry before overpiping with a No2 nozzle. When piping these lines, remember to anchor the beginning of the icing by touching the tip of the nozzle against the cake as you start to pipe, then lift the nozzle and, keeping a constant pressure on the bag, let the icing fall out of the nozzle until you reach an angle or point at which you wish to stop. If you release the pressure on the bag, the icing will stop being pushed out so simply touch the surface once more with the point of the nozzle. Tidy up any irregularities in the line with a damp paintbrush. One of the main points to watch when piping lines is not to begin pushing the icing out of the nozzle too quickly, or the line will start with a large blob.

Using a No2 nozzle, pipe a small shell or teardrop edging along the outer edge of the design. With a No3 nozzle, pipe lines of five shells on the top edge of the cake between the stippled designs, then pipe a border of shells around the bottom edge of the cake. On a 25-cm (10-in) square cake, you should aim to pipe approximately 25 shells on each side.

Trim the sides of the cake board with silver banding, then secure the small silver rings and slippers to the cake with a little royal icing.

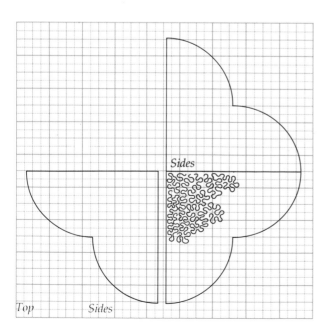

Lovebirds

Ingredients
15-cm (6-in) square fruit cake
20-cm (8-in) square fruit cake
25-cm (10-in) square fruit cake
boiled sieved apricot jam or egg white
3kg (6lb 8oz) marzipan
water or alcohol
2.5kg (5lb 8oz) royal icing
400g (14oz) royal icing for piping
violet food colouring or violet petal dust
125g (4oz) pastillage

Equipment
22.5-cm (9-in) square cake board
27.5-cm (11-in) square cake board
35-cm (14-in) square cake board
tracing paper
white card
waxed paper
No0 nozzle
No1 nozzle
No2 nozzle
No3 nozzle
No5 nozzle for pastillage card
vegetable parchment piping bags
cranked palette knife or paintbrush
silver banding
scriber
8 8.75-cm (3½-in) round plaster cake pillars
5-cm (2-in) heart-shaped cutter for pastillage
   card
selection of food colouring pens for pastillage
   card
½ metre (½ yard) 3-mm (⅛-in) violet satin
   ribbon for pastillage card

Number of portions
160-170

Amount of work involved
Approximately 9 hours

The extensive use of lace pieces, and the application of handmade corner ornaments, known as off pieces, to this quite simple royal iced cake, shows the type of work you can achieve once you've got a little experience. It is very time-consuming piping the quantity of lace that is required (see page 24), and to decorate all three tiers you will need about 10 sheets — between 450 and 500 pieces in all, so begin piping these at the earliest possible moment! Here, the lace is made partly from white royal icing, but the tips of each piece are completed in pale violet to match other parts of the cake. You

can do this either by using two bags of royal icing, one white and one violet, or the lace can be piped completely in white and then very carefully dusted with violet petal dust when it is dry. In either case use a No0 nozzle.

To pipe the S-shaped corner pieces, use the template provided to trace 12 S-shapes on to sheets of white card and cover them with pieces of waxed paper. Using a No3 nozzle and violet-coloured royal icing, pipe over the outlines, then leave to dry. With a No2 nozzle, pipe a series of small shells or teardrops down one side of each outline and leave to dry. When hardened, carefully remove the S-shapes from the waxed paper and turn them over, then pipe another series of shells or teardrops down the outlines. You can work on the lace and off pieces between applying coats of royal icing to the cakes themselves, to ensure that no time is wasted.

Prepare the cakes in the usual way and coat each cake board with a thin layer of royal icing, leave to dry and then trim the edges with silver banding. Using a No2 nozzle and white royal icing, on the top of each cake pipe straight lines running parallel at a distance of 2.5cm (1in) from the edges of the cakes. Leave to dry, then overpipe the lines with a No1 nozzle. With a No0 nozzle, pipe cornelli work (see page 17) to the border area on the top of each cake. Now pipe the shell, or teardrop, border around the top and bottom of each cake, using a No2 or No1 nozzle. Then pipe the vertical line of shells down the corner of each cake. Overpipe two lines, running parallel to the shell borders, on each cake board, using a No2 nozzle to pipe the lower line and overpiping it with a No1 nozzle, then pipe the whole of the exposed boards with a delicate layer of cornelli work, using a No0 nozzle. Leave to dry.

To pipe the half-relief lovebirds on to the sides of

the cakes, copy the template provided on to tracing paper, then use it to scribe the outlines of the birds in the centre of the side of each cake. Using a No1 nozzle and white royal icing, pipe the back wings, tail feathers and details of the twigs the birds are carrying. The front wings are piped as off pieces on to waxed paper and must be dry before the rest of the bird is piped. Pipe a teardrop sideways to form the head and beak of each bird, then pipe the body as a larger teardrop trailing away towards the tail. While the body is still soft, place the front wing in position at a 45° angle to the body, so that it stands out from the side of the cake. Leave to dry.

On any cake it is important to ensure that lacework is evenly spaced and uniformly positioned, and on this cake, where the lace is angular and stands up from its outer edges, it is especially important. To attach the lace to the top of the cake, using a No1 nozzle pipe a fine line of royal icing, 12mm (½in) long, just behind the border of shells or teardrops. Remove each piece of lace from its backing sheet of waxed paper using a cranked palette knife or paintbrush, and position it in the wet icing with your fingers. When the upper rows of lace are in place, position the lower rows against the overpiped rows of icing 6mm (¼in) from the edge of each cake, so that the lace stands proud of the sides of each cake. Leave to dry. To finish the cake, secure the S-shaped off pieces to the corners of each cake, applying royal icing at the three points where the curves are in contact with the board or the cake.

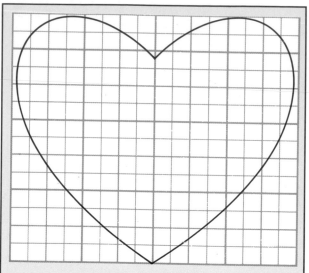

Making a pastillage card

Dust a flat surface with cornflour (cornstarch), then roll out a sheet of pastillage or petal paste until it is 1.5mm ($^1/_{16}$in) thick and, while it is still soft and pliable, cut out two rectangular pieces about 10 x 7.5cm (4 x 3in). In one of them, cut out a heart shape using a tinplate cutter, or the template provided, which you then discard, and in both pieces cut two holes down one side, about 6mm (¼in) in diameter, through which the silk bow is to be threaded when the card is assembled. When the pastillage is dry, paint or draw your chosen design on the solid rectangular card. Edible food colouring pens are ideal for this. On the other card, decorate the outline of the heart with dots of icing and a small scallop design piped around the outside edge. Cut small flowers from a piece of violet-coloured pastillage and attach them to the front of the card with royal icing, then join the two pieces together with a length of loosely tied ribbon. Measure the length of the bottom edge of the card and pipe two straight lines of shells in a V-shape on the top of the smallest cake, then set the base of the card into this icing while it is still wet. Tighten the ribbon bow and strengthen the hinge side of the card by joining both parts with a line of shells piped with a No5 nozzle. Finish the front of the card by piping two lovebirds at the bottom corners of the card.

Making lace pieces

To make the large quantities of lace needed to decorate a three-tier cake, you must draw the lace pattern on to a card so that the pattern is repeated many times. Six columns of nine or ten pieces will fit easily on to a postcard. Secure the card to a rigid surface, then cover it with a sheet of waxed tissue paper, shiny side uppermost. Now pipe on to the paper directly over each pattern, following the outline and ensuring that all the lines that are meant to touch really do so. These are what give the lace its strength. When you have filled the sheet, remove it carefully and place it in a safe place to dry — a shallow cardboard box is ideal. Place another sheet of waxed paper over the lace templates and repeat the procedure until you have piped the required number of pieces. If you are making coloured lace it is a good idea to pipe it all from one batch of icing at a time, or you may have difficulty matching the colours later. If piping multi-coloured lace, use two or three bags of icing to pipe a row of each colour. Alternatively, the finished lace can be dusted with petal dust.

Using a No0 nozzle, or a larger one, is quite straightforward, but if you wish to make really fine lace with a No00 nozzle the icing string may break as a result of blockages in the nozzle. If this happens, beat the icing vigorously and use a fresh nozzle and bag. If that fails the problem may lie with the icing itself, in which case you must make a fresh batch using the finest grade of icing (confectioner's) sugar and sieving it through a very fine mesh sieve (ideally brass, of laboratory quality).

Ribbons and bells

This cake calls for expertise, patience and a steady hand, but the spectacular results are well worth the effort, and make a very unusual and attractive wedding cake.

Cover the cakes with a layer of marzipan and sugarpaste in the usual way and leave to dry. Cover each cake board with a sheet of patterned silver paper, then place each cake on its board. Make the runout bells *(see page 27)* and leave to dry. Trace the patterns for the lace, extension work and embroidery on to sheets of tracing paper, then scribe the outlines on to the sides of the cakes. Using a No0 or No1 nozzle and royal icing, pipe a fine line of beading, or snail trail, around the base of each cake and leave to dry. Using a softened icing (thinner than normal royal icing, but slightly thicker than a flooding icing), begin to work on the wide ribbons. Because they are quite small, there is no need to pipe an outline around them, and the width and depth of the lines depends entirely on the amount of icing applied. Use a fine sable paintbrush to push the icing into the points and to smooth it until it is level. When doing this type of direct flooding you may find it helpful to tilt the cake away from you slightly to stop the icing running down the side of the cake. Complete the rest of the embroidery, then attach the runout bells to the sides of the cakes with a little royal icing.

On most cakes where the extension work is arranged in tiers, it is usual to begin by piping the bridgework — the scalloped pattern which supports the vertical lines of extension — for the lowest level first. Begin by working on the bridgework for one of the corner arrangements, and with deep apricot-coloured royal icing of piping consistency and a No0 or No1 nozzle, follow the scalloped scribed outline to pipe the first row of icing. Repeat the process on each corner. Return to the starting point and begin piping the next line directly against the first, so that when completed you will have two rows standing out horizontally from the cake like a narrow platform. If the icing strand does not adhere to the one already in position, you can sometimes encourage it to stick with a moistened paintbrush — a fine sable watercolourist's No0 or No1 is best. Begin piping the third row about 6mm (¼in) from the end of the lines already piped and make it shorter by the same distance. The fourth, fifth and sixth rows are also each piped shorter than the last by the same amount. The seventh row is piped to the full length of the first and second. If the bridgework seems very weak, it can be reinforced so that it will support the extension piping or curtain work by using a No3 sable paintbrush and very diluted royal icing, of the consistency of clear honey, and painting over the scallops.

When the bridgework is complete on each corner of the cake, prepare the cake icing immedi-

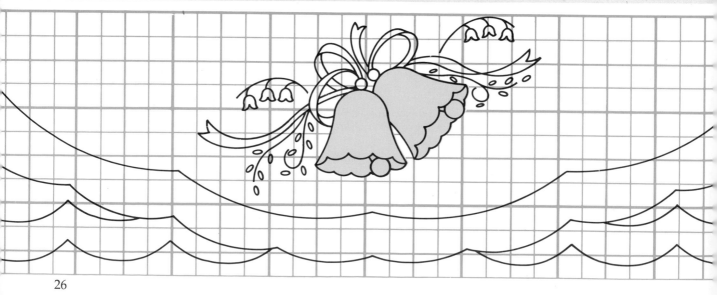

ately above it by tinting it with petal dust and cornflour (cornstarch) mixed together to achieve the right shade. Use tangerine petal dust to colour the cake behind the lower two bands of extension and orange sparkle behind the upper extension band. Use a small, soft, dry brush to transfer the colour to the cake and apply it with a stippling action, taking care not to damage the bridgework.

Before piping the vertical extension work, pipe the first row of the upper corner bridgework with a slightly lighter shade of apricot-coloured royal icing. Using this shade and a No00 nozzle, begin piping the lower extension. Complete each strand by lightly touching the tip of the icing nozzle against the side of the cake, squeezing the bag and drawing it smoothly towards the bridge itself. Stop squeezing after you have passed the bridgework to cut off the flow of icing. Do not touch the bridgework with the tip of the nozzle or you could break it. When you have piped two or three vertical lines, use a damp fine paintbrush to wipe away any excess icing which may be left hanging below the edge of the bridge. Remember that this is a precision job and that extension work can be easily broken. When the lower band of extension work is complete, apply the same technique to pipe the middle band, but use a paler apricot-coloured royal icing for the vertical strands and for the bridgework of the upper band of extension which passes right round each tier. The upper band of vertical extension is piped with white royal icing, but because of the shading behind it, it looks pale apricot in colour. When all the extension work is finished, pipe a row of fine scallops, or very small dropped loops, along the edge of the bridgework in order to cover any ends of the vertical strands of icing.

The lacework (see page 24) is piped with a No00 or No0 nozzle in three sizes, with the smallest pieces for the top tier and the largest pieces for the bottom one, using the template provided. You will require approximately 100-120 pieces for the bottom tier, about 80-100 pieces for the middle and 50-70 pieces for the top. Attach each piece to the cake with a fine piped line about 6mm (¼in) long, just above the top of the vertical extension. Remove each piece of lace from the waxed paper on which it was piped with a flexible thin-bladed palette knife, but actually place it against the cake with your fingertips. Ensure that each piece is set at the same angle of about 45° from the side.

Since the tiers of the cake are supported on simple clear acrylic stands, there is no need to prepare the tops of the cakes for supports in any way, and the flower arrangements, whether in sugar or silk, can be prepared at any time and placed in the centre of each acrylic stand. Make the pastillage bell (see page 34), decorate the bottom edge with a No1 crimper and carefully bore a hole through the top while the paste is still soft, then thread through a short length of wire or knotted ribbon in order to be able to hang it in place.

Making the runout bells

Four sets of bells, two facing in each direction, are required for each tier. You will need some sheets of waxed paper, a flat board or a piece of glass on to which the runouts are piped, and a small bowl of flooding royal icing. After tracing the designs on to a sheet of paper, fix this paper to the flat board with a dab of icing or small piece of sticky tape. Place a sheet of waxed paper, shiny side up, over the board and secure it in place. Use a bag of apricot-coloured icing of normal piping consistency and pipe around the outline of the bells with a No0 nozzle. Now fill a piping bag with the same colour icing weakened to a flooding consistency — thin enough to be brushed smooth after being squeezed from the bag, but not thin enough to flow of its own accord. Cut the tip from the end of the bag to leave a hole about the size of a No2 nozzle, and gently squeeze the icing on to the waxed paper and flood the area of the base or mouth of each bell. Leave to dry.

Now take a second bag and fill it with a slightly lighter shade of apricot-coloured icing and, holding the tip of the bag in the icing, move it from side to side across the lower bell. This helps to push the icing right up to the piped border. With practice you will be able to fill the enclosed area completely until the icing is just about to escape over the top of the outline. Use a fine sable paintbrush to ensure that the outline is covered by the flooding icing. If you have an adjustable electric lamp, shine it on to the freshly flooded bell from a distance of about 30cm (12in). The heat it produces will encourage the surface of the icing to form a crust quickly and give it a pleasing sheen. After 10 minutes, or as soon as the icing has crusted over, flood the second bell on top. About an hour later, or when the bells are dry enough, with a No00 nozzle, pipe the contrasting scalloped outline in white icing around the rim of each bell, the fine embroidery design on each bell and pipe the clappers. Then place the work in an airing cupboard for at least 24 hours to dry out. Do not remove the waxed paper until you intend to attach the bells to the cake.

To remove the bells from the waxed paper, detach the paper from the backing board and slide it to the edge, until the side of the flooding just overlaps it. Now peel the paper downwards and away from the back of the icing. Allow the paper to move gradually across the board, while maintaining an even pressure on the side that you are pulling, until the entire flooding work has been released. Alternatively, if the flooded pieces are small, they can be lifted off with a thin-bladed cranked palette knife.

Hearts and flowers

Ingredients

17.5-cm (7-in) heart-shaped fruit cake
25-cm (10-in) heart-shaped fruit cake
32.5-cm (13-in) heart-shaped fruit cake
boiled sieved apricot jam or egg white
3.6kg (8lb) marzipan
water or alcohol
4.8kg (10lb) sugarpaste
475g (1lb 1oz) royal icing
black food colouring
chestnut food colouring
Cornish cream food colouring
rose food colouring
skintone food colouring

Equipment

22.5-cm (9-in) heart-shaped cake board
30-cm (12-in) heart-shaped cake board
40-cm (16-in) heart-shaped cake board
4 metres (4½ yards) 12-mm (½-in)
  silver banding
No0 plain nozzle
No5 shell nozzle
vegetable parchment piping bags
tracing paper
scriber
6 large open sugar roses
18 pink sugar blossom sprays
11 cream sugar blossoms with pink stamens
10 cream sugar blossoms with cream stamens
rose petal cutter
set of 3 blossom plunger cutters
pink plain round stamens
cream round pearl stamens
pointed cream stamens
10 metres (11 yards) 3-mm (⅛-in) double-sided
  cream ribbon
6 metres (6½ yards) 3-mm (⅛-in) double-sided
  pink ribbon
5 metres (5½ yards) 8-mm (⅜-in) acetate satin
  cream ribbon
3 x 8.75-cm (3½-in) silver octagonal pillars
3 x 7.5-cm (3-in) silver octagonal pillars
No4 crimper for plaque

Number of portions
180-200

Amount of work involved
Approximately 20 hours

A heart-shaped cake is extremely popular for weddings and is surprisingly easy to cut into portions. This cake calls for a range of decorating techniques with which you should be familiar before beginning work. The effectiveness of this ivory-coloured design depends on the care with which the major decorations are arranged to provide a visual balance, and on each of the lower tiers the pairs of quite large pastillage roses and their filler flowers and ribbons are offset against minute piped sugar doves and a few more flowers.

The day before you plan to begin work on the cake, mix some Cornish cream food colouring with the sugarpaste until you get an even tone, then leave in an air-tight container for 24 hours. Cover the cakes with marzipan and sugarpaste in the usual way, then position each one on its cake board. Using a No5 shell nozzle and royal icing, pipe a line of shells around the bottom edges of each cake and leave to dry. Attach silver banding to each board. Make the lace *(see page 24)* and leave to dry. Make templates of the embroidery, then scribe the outlines of the pattern around the sides of each cake. You may find this easiest when the cake is placed on a turntable. Using a No0 nozzle and royal icing, work on one cake at a time, beginning at the highest point of the pattern. Turn the cake in a clockwise direction if you are right-handed, and work from left to right. If you are left-handed, it may be easiest to begin in the same place but to turn the cake in an anti-clockwise direction. The stem lines of the embroidery are piped keeping the tip of the nozzle just off the icing and following the scribed lines in one fluid movement. The heart shape is piped in a series of bulbs of icing, starting with the smaller ones at the top and graduating to larger ones on the sides. Remember to take the nozzle off to the side after releasing the pressure on the piping bag and before removing the tip from the bulb of icing to avoid creating a point on the top of each bulb. The small flowers are piped by building up three circular layers of icing to form a hollow flower, and the pale pink forget-me-nots are piped as a series of five dots of icing, with another one in the centre. Leave to dry.

Arrange open roses, with pink and cream blossom sprays, on the bottom and middle tiers. Place the other blossom sprays on the top tier, and arrange the pastillage heart *(see page 30)* on top of them and at an angle. Use thinly piped curved lines of royal icing to attach the pieces of lace to the sides of each cake, gently arranging them beneath each segment of embroidery. Leave to dry, then very carefully pipe a scalloped line just above each piece of lace. This draws the eye around each cake to unify the piped designs. Assemble the cakes, using the larger pillars to support the medium tier, and the smaller pillars to support the top one.

Making the heart-shaped plaque

Prepare a pastillage or sugarpaste plaque two or three days in advance to allow it harden. However, the edges of the heart are decorated with a No4 crimper while the paste is still soft. Trace the design on to tracing paper, place on top of the plaque and scribe around the main outlines. Fill a piping bag with flooding royal icing and, holding the tip of the bag close to the surface of the plaque, squeeze the bag with your thumb to force out the icing. Keep the pointed end of the bag in the icing and move it from side to side to disperse it. If necessary, use a fine sable paintbrush to ease the icing up to the outlines of the design and to disperse any air bubbles. Work from the background to the foreground. To create folds in the bride's dress, pipe alternate sections of her skirt and allow them to dry partially or crust over, then fill in the missing sections. If you wish to use very strong colours, such as red or black, pipe the light colours first and allow them to dry completely before applying the deeply coloured icing, otherwise the colour will bleed into the adjacent pale-coloured areas. Once you have finished the flooding, leave the plaque to dry in an airing cupboard or a box filled with silica gel crystals. To make the bride's head dress, brush transparently thin flooding royal icing over the area of the veil and leave to dry, then pipe a scalloped edge around the veil with a No0 nozzle. Very small pink and cream blossom flowers for the bouquet and head dress are cut from pastillage and attached with royal icing. Then paint in the details with a very fine paintbrush and liquid food colouring.

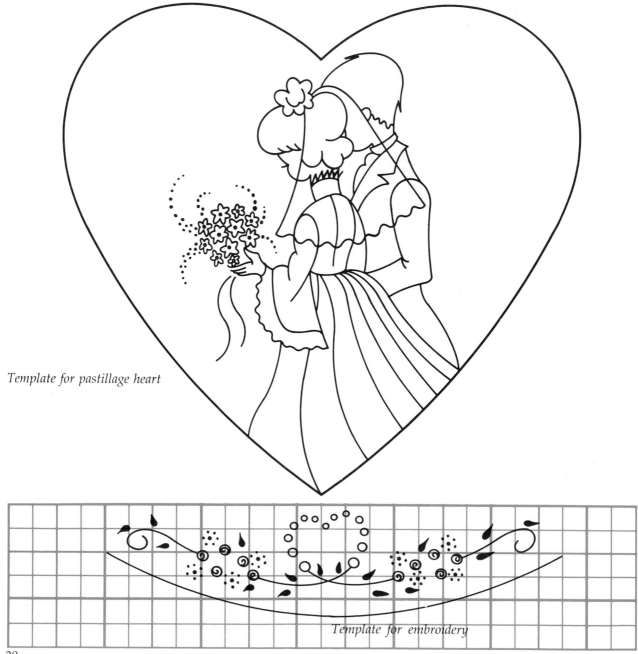

Template for pastillage heart

Template for embroidery

Swan upping

Ingredients
17.5-cm (7-in) heart-shaped fruit cake
25-cm (10-in) heart-shaped fruit cake
boiled sieved apricot jam or egg white
1.7kg (3lb 11oz) marzipan
water or alcohol
1.7kg (3lb 11oz) royal icing
625g (1lb 6oz) royal icing for piping
black food colouring
orange food colouring

Equipment
25-cm (10-in) heart-shaped cake board
35-cm (14-in) heart-shaped cake board
tracing paper
scriber
No0 nozzle
No1 nozzle
No3 nozzle
No42 nozzle
vegetable parchment piping bags
waxed tissue paper
masking tape
2 metres (2¼ yards) 3-mm (⅛-in) double-sided
   lemon satin ribbon
3 20-cm (8-in) wooden skewers
3 8.75-cm (3½-in) octagonal plastic pillars
paintbrush
8 sugar blossoms wired into sprays
4 metres (4½ yards) 8-mm (⅜-in) sealed-edge
   lemon acetate satin ribbon
set of 3 blossom plunger cutters

Number of portions
90-95

Amount of work involved
Approximately 5½ hours

One of the most graceful elements of traditional royal iced cake designs is the use of sugar to make wafer-thin collars which then rest above or against the sides of an otherwise conventionally iced cake. It is possible to create designs of great variety and complexity, but here simple, and comparatively strong, collars have been used, placed directly in contact with the tops of the cakes. Note that the same design is reflected in the runout icing used on the cakeboards to balance the overhang of the collar from the side of the cake.

Cover each cake with marzipan and royal icing in the usual way, then coat each cake board with white royal icing and leave to dry. Using the template, pipe the simple embroidery pattern around the sides of each cake with a No1 nozzle.

To make the runout collars, you will need two sheets of waxed tissue paper; a flat board or piece of glass to fit beneath each piece of waxed paper; a dry, not humid, room in which to work and an airing cupboard for storage; a portable anglepoise, or similar lamp, with which you can direct gentle heat on to the runouts to help in their initial drying and to encourage a slightly glossy surface finish; royal icing made 24 hours in advance and softened to a flooding consistency but not containing any glycerine, which would weaken the runouts.

To make the collars, trace the full-size template on to a sheet of paper and secure it at the corners to the flat board with masking tape. Attach the waxed paper, shiny side up, to the top of the drawings in a similar manner. Do not tape right round, or you may trap air underneath the waxed paper. Now cut a small cross in the centre of the paper but do not cut close to the collar itself. This allows the paper to relax when the wet icing is applied and contract as the icing dries out without distorting the collar itself.

Fit a small piping bag with a No1 nozzle, then half-fill it with normal royal icing of a piping consistency, and fill two or three larger bags half-full of softened royal icing of flooding strength. Pipe unbroken lines along the outlines of the collar with the No1 nozzle. Next, take one of the larger filled bags, and cut off the tip of the cone to leave a hole equivalent in size to a No3 nozzle. Flood the icing up to the piped edges of the design, keeping the point of the bag in the icing all the time to eliminate any air bubbles. Work from a given point 5-7.5-cm (2-3-in) to the left, then 5-7.5-cm (2-3-in) to the right, repeating the process, further to the left, then further to the right. By working in alternate sections until the outline is completely filled in, it is unlikely that any part of the collar will have begun to dry significantly before the adjoining section is completed. Use a soft paintbrush to disperse the icing and to push it up to and just on to the edge of the piped linework.

Allow the floodings to dry for at least 48 hours, then pipe the decorative embroidery and six-point lace using a No0 nozzle. The lace is made by piping three dots of icing, leaving a space, then piping three more dots of icing and so on, right around the collar, making sure that each dot is fixed to the side of the collar. These will dry quite quickly, and by the time you have completed the first row, the second row of two dots can be piped and then the third row of single dots. Again make sure that each dot is touching its neighbour.

The flooded base border around the base of each tier is a direct runout on to the iced surface of the board. Work on this piece after the cake has been placed in position, coated and dried. Use a template to mark the position of the collar, then pipe an outline using a No1 nozzle. Flood and decorate the base collars with a similar design to that on the upper ones and leave to dry. Pipe a line of beading around the base of each cake, using a No42 nozzle. Leave to dry, then secure the 3-mm (⅛-in) ribbon around each cake.

The hardest part of the operation is the removal of the collar from its waxed paper backing. Leave the runout on its backing board and place it on a turntable. Loosen the paper from the backing board and slide it gently until one edge of the runout just projects over the edge of the board. Take hold of the paper and pull it steadily downwards, peeling it away from the collar until about half the collar has been released. Rotate the turntable and repeat the process until the entire runout is free. Move the collar as little as possible until you are ready to place it on the cake.

Once all the direct piping on to the cake has been completed, pipe a continuous line of icing or shells, using a No3 nozzle, around the top edge of each cake. Supporting the collar with both hands, place it gently on the top of the iced line. If there is a gap between the collar and the cake top, pipe a line of beading along the inside edge with a No0 nozzle. Finish the join by piping a similar line of beading below the outer edge of the collar where it rests against the side of the cake.

The swan centre piece is made by a similar runout method to the collar, except that the head, neck and body of the swan are double-flooded. This means that after the normal flooding coating has dried and been removed from its waxed paper backing, it is turned over and a second layer of icing is flooded directly on to the dried section. This is also allowed to dry, and is subsequently painted with orange and black food colouring to indicate such details as the beak and the eyes.

Pipe the wings, using a No3 nozzle and royal

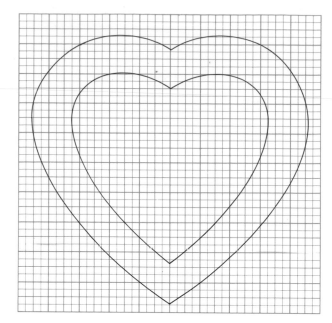

icing that is stiff, not a flooding consistency, on to waxed paper. Leave the icing heavily textured, to represent the wing feathers. Begin at the base of the wing, and pipe in the direction of the arrows on the template. Leave to dry. Remove the wings from the waxed paper and assemble the swan on the dried royal icing base by piping a line of shells to support the body. Attach each wing at a slight angle to the body with a bead of royal icing at the base of each wing. If necessary, place temporary supports of cotton wool or sponge rubber under the wings until the icing dries. Then remove the supports and fill the area behind the neck and between the wings with a little sugarpaste. Press flowers and ribbons into the paste, and arrange them over the wings. Do not place the swan in position on the cake until the last moment, as the neck is fragile and easily damaged.

Wedding bells

Ingredients
15-cm (6-in) hexagonal fruit cake
20-cm (8-in) hexagonal fruit cake
boiled sieved apricot jam or egg white
1.2kg (2lb 12oz) marzipan
water or alcohol
900g (2lb) royal icing
225g (8oz) royal icing for piping
125g (4oz) pastillage
cornflour (cornstarch)

Equipment
20-cm (8-in) hexagonal cake board
30-cm (12-in) hexagonal cake board
No1 nozzle
No5 nozzle
No11 nozzle
vegetable parchment piping bags
1 medium bell mould
1 large bell mould
cranked palette or fine craft knife
No1 or No2 scallop crimper
4 metres (4½ yards) 12-mm (½-in) lace-edged
   white iridescent ribbon
florists' wire
1 half-relief chocolate moulding bell mould
collapsible acrylic cake stand

Number of portions
60-65

Amount of work involved
Approximately 3½ hours

This elegant cake may look complicated but in fact it is ideal for an inexperienced cake decorator to attempt with confidence. Only a limited amount of piping skill is required, and once the cakes have been coated with a minimum of three coats of icing, the decoration and finishing should not take more than about two hours.

Ice the cakes in the usual way. Leave to dry, then place on silver cake boards. Using a No11 nozzle and white royal icing, pipe a large shell at each of the bottom corners of the two cakes, then pipe a line of shells connecting each corner piece. Pipe a border of shells around the top edges of each cake, then pipe a vertical line of shells, using a No5 nozzle, down the corners of each cake. Using a No1 nozzle and working on the cake boards, pipe three dots leading from each corner shell to the edge of the board.

To make the hollow bells, take a clean dry bell mould and dust the inside liberally with cornflour (cornstarch). Roll out a piece of pastillage so that it is at least 12-mm (½-in) thick and just bigger than the mouth of the bell mould. Gently press the paste down into the well of the bell, ensuring that it does not stick to the mould. Do not try to push the paste all the way into the base straight away. Take the paste out and dust the mould again with cornflour, replace the paste in the mould and push down a little further. Repeat this three or four times until you can feel the base of the mould through the paste. Then smooth some of the paste away from the base and back up the sides of the mould towards the mouth, rotating the bell and working the paste until it has stretched out to form a lining inside the mould. At intervals, remove the paste from the mould to redust it with cornflour. Try to make the lining as thin as possible without tearing it.

Trim off any excess paste with a cranked palette or fine craft knife. While the paste is still pliable, trim the edges to a scallop shape using a No1 or No2 scallop crimper, cutting through the paste to the mould. If the walls of the bell are very thin, the finished result will look more attractive and will dry more quickly than if it is left a little thicker. Make sure the bell can be released easily from the mould before putting it aside to dry, still in the mould, which should be left in an upright position. After about one hour in warm, dry conditions, the bell can be turned out and then left overnight to dry completely. For this cake you will need two large bells and three medium ones. If you wish, you can decorate the mouths of these bells with a simple embroidery pattern which is piped freehand with a No1 nozzle. An example of the type of pattern which is suitable for this is shown below. Decorate the exterior of each bell with cornelli piping *(see page 17)*.

Finish each bell by dressing it with a few ribbon

Embroidery inside mouth of bells

34

loops and a clapper made from a ball of sugarpaste held in position with a piece of florists' wire. If you wish, you can use ribbons in colours which harmonise with the dresses of the bride or brides-maids. Decorate the rim of each bell with a line of beading piped with a No1 nozzle.

Make the half-relief mouldings for the sides of the cake with pastillage and a sheet of half-relief bells. Lightly dust each mould with cornflour, then roll out a small piece of pastillage until it is about 12-mm (½-in) thick and press it into the moulds. Cut off any excess paste with a cranked palette or fine craft knife, working from the inside of each mould to the outside in order to achieve a flat base and a sharp edge to the moulding. Before leaving

the moulds to dry, make sure that the pastillage can be released by tapping the edge on the work surface. If you have dusted the inside of the moulds well with the cornflour, the pastillage should just fall out. If you have any difficulty getting it out, lift one corner of the paste with the point of your knife and peel it from the mould. This may distort the shape so dust the mould again and replace the pastillage.

When the bells are hard enough to handle, release them from their moulds and fix them to the sides of the cakes with small amounts of royal icing, then arrange the hollow bells on the top of each cake. Place the smaller cake on the acrylic stand.

Happy ever after

Ingredients
15-cm (6-in) hexagonal fruit cake
2 25-cm (10-in) hexagonal fruit cakes
boiled sieved apricot jam or egg white
2.9kg (6lb 4oz) marzipan
water or alcohol
3.25kg (7lb 2oz) sugarpaste
50g (2oz) royal icing
cornflour (cornstarch)

Equipment
20-cm (8-in) hexagonal cake board
2 30-cm (12-in) hexagonal cake boards
tracing paper
white card
No23 classic crimper
embossing tool
8 metres (8¾ yards) 3-mm (⅛-in) double-sided
   dusty pink satin ribbon
8 metres (8¾ yards) 3-mm (⅛-in) double-sided
   silver grey satin ribbon
10 metres (11 yards) 8-mm (⅜-in) cut-edge
   white acetate satin ribbon
8 jasmine pink silk flowers
8 pink silk blossoms
6 large white silk roses
8 wired silver leaves
36 unwired small silver leaves
36 small pink single blossoms
8 sprays of white silk bellflowers
commercial bride and groom caketop figures
parafilm or florists' tape
white-coated 24 gauge wire
4 20-cm (8-in) wooden skewers
4 8.75-cm (3½-in) octagonal silver plastic cake
   pillars

Number of portions
150-160

Amount of time involved
Approximately 4 hours

This pretty cake is extremely simple and quick to prepare, but looks very effective. Only commercial decorations are used, and there is no piping work, so it would be an ideal cake to make at the last minute for a whirlwind wedding!

To stop the sugarpaste drying out before you are ready to use it, work on one cake at a time, wrapping the remaining sugarpaste in a plastic bag and placing it inside an air-tight container. Cover the cake with a layer of marzipan and one of sugarpaste in the usual way, working on the sugarpaste until it is completely smooth, and then decorate it with the various patterns. Here, the embossed patterns are applied with a cake decorator's embossing tool, but many craft embossing tools will also give pleasing effects.

To mark the limits of the area to be embossed, make a V-shaped template in white card from the pattern provided, then hold it flat against the sugarpaste with one hand while pressing against its top edge to leave a faint indentation in the icing. This acts as a guideline when you impress the pattern of the crimper jaws into the surface. Do not press too hard with the crimper, or you will cut right through the paste to the marzipan beneath. Some cake decorators find it easier to hold the crimper jaws open in one position by fixing a rubber band around them so that they cannot open too far. The secret of good crimping is to work at eye level and to take your time in positioning the crimpers before pushing them into sugarpaste. If you make a mistake, gently rub the pattern out using the palm of your hand and then smooth it over with an icing smoother.

After you have crimped right around the cake, press the embossing tool gently against the sugarpaste to leave a clearly defined impression when the tool is withdrawn. Be careful to keep the end of the embosser always at the same angle, and keep the impressions evenly spaced while working steadily around the cake. If the embossing tool sticks in the sugarpaste, dust the end with a little cornflour (cornstarch), but be careful not to block up the indentations or you will lose the sharpness of the pattern on the cake. Repeat the process for the other two cakes, then leave them for at least 24 hours to allow the sugarpaste to harden.

Using the template provided, cut out a hexagonal pad of sugarpaste about 10-cm (4-in) wide and 12-mm (½-in) thick on which the figures of the bride and groom will stand. Decorate the edges with the crimper. Neatly wrap a piece of dusty pink ribbon around the bottom edge of each cake to conceal any irregularity in the icing where it has been trimmed.

You can have the silk flowers made into sprays for you, or you can wire them together yourself and set them into a small pad of sugarpaste which is then placed in position. Never push the wires directly into the cake. Using dabs of royal icing position a silk flower on each side of each cake, setting it just above the crimped V-shape.

To make the inward arching columns of flowers on either side of the bride and groom, take a selection of small blossoms and nylon-threaded pearl loops and bind them with parafilm, or florists' tape, to a piece of white-coated 24 gauge wire. Form the curved shapes by hand and set the bases into the hexagonal sugarpaste pad.

Although it looks as though only two pillars

have been used to support the upper tier, there are in fact four. Two pillars are placed on each base cake, with one on each side of the spray of flowers. When setting the pillars on this cake, be careful not to place them so close to the edges of the lower tier that they only pierce the marzipan. The wooden supporting skewers must penetrate the fruit cake themselves if the columns are to be sufficiently strong to support the upper tier.

Template to indicate the extent of the embossing patterns, and hexagonal template for the top-piece

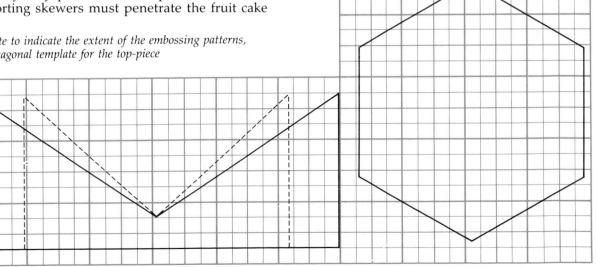

Winter wedding

Ingredients
15-cm (6-in) hexagonal fruit cake
25-cm (10-in) hexagonal fruit cake
boiled sieved apricot jam or egg white
1.7kg (3lb 14oz) marzipan
water or alcohol
2kg (4lb 8oz) royal icing
450g (1lb) royal icing for piping
gum tragacanth
25g (1oz) red dragées
apple green food colouring
jade green food colouring
moss green food colouring

Equipment
25-cm (10-in) hexagonal cake board
30-cm (12-in) hexagonal cake board
velvet ribbon
No1 nozzle
No0 nozzle
No2 nozzle
vegetable parchment piping bags
tracing paper
waxed tissue paper
paintbrush
50g (2oz) leaf gelatine or 1 sheet cellophane
scissors
white card
paper clip
foam rubber
8 sugar Christmas roses
10 large sugar holly leaves
12 small sugar holly leaves
8 large sugar ivy leaves
12 small sugar ivy leaves
8 extra small plastic horseshoes
½ metre (½ yard) 3-mm (⅛-in) white ribbon
6 medium plastic horseshoes

Number of portions
85-95

Amount of work involved
Approximately 10½ hours

Without doubt, the most popular time of year for weddings is during the spring and early summer, although of course weddings are celebrated throughout the year! However, choosing a seasonal theme for a winter wedding can be quite difficult. If you do use holly be careful how to apply it, since it has a very distinctive leaf form that is more widely associated with Christmas celebrations than weddings.

Ice the cakes and boards with royal icing in the usual way and leave to dry. Trim the edges of the boards with velvet ribbon. Pipe a double line of beading, arranged to look like herringbone, around the top and bottom edges of each cake, using a No1 nozzle for the top tier and a No2 nozzle for the lower one. Ensure that the beading is perfectly straight, so as to conceal any irregularities at the edges.

To make the frames for the windows, trace the templates provided on to a large sheet of paper. You will need two individual side windows and one large window for the top piece, and six three-piece sets in each of the two sizes. Prepare some extra pieces to allow for breakages. Fix the drawings to a flat board and cover with a piece of waxed tissue paper, securing it in place with dots of royal icing or a little sticky tape. With a No0 nozzle carefully pipe over the outlines of the window. Using flooding icing (see page 27), fortified with gum tragacanth for extra strength, fill in the framework between the piped lines, working the icing with a damp paintbrush to disperse the air bubbles. Leave to dry for 24 hours.

The stained glass windows are made from leaf gelatine, which is generally available from continental delicatessens and good cake decoration shops. One manufacturer supplies his standard product with a diamond pattern across the sheets, which are approximately 25 x 7.5cm (10 x 3in), which means you can achieve the leaded glass effect without even trying. All gelatine is highly susceptible to moisture, and the sheets of gelatine can buckle and distort very easily, so take care where you leave the finished window pieces! In its natural form, leaf gelatine is transparent and almost colourless, so if you wish to give it emphasis when placed on the cake, you will have to tint it, using the minimum amount of moisture. The best method is to spray the food colouring from an aerosol can or in an airbrush, if you have one. Spray both sides of the gelatine, coating the second side immediately after the first, as this will prevent the sheets curling too much. They may distort a little, but they will become flat again as they dry out and within half an hour they will be dry enough to be cut out with scissors. First cut out the template for the window from a piece of stiff card or plastic and secure it behind the gelatine with a paper clip. Don't push the paper clip

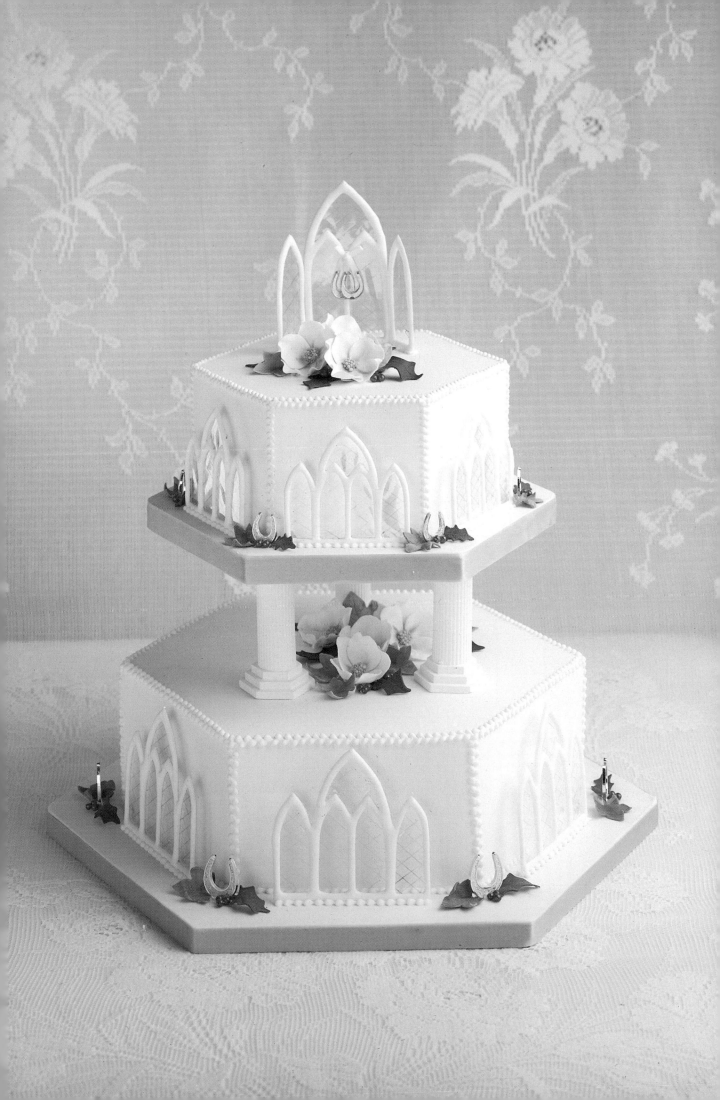

completely home, as you can manipulate the gelatine together with the templates as you cut round its edge with scissors. Try not to handle the front or back of the gelatine leaves as fingerprints show up very quickly.

Remove the hardened piped frames from their backing sheets and place them face down on a thin piece of foam rubber. Then pipe a double line of royal icing down the centre of each part of the frame and carefully place the leaf gelatine in position, pressing it with only just enough force to make it stick against the wet icing. Even at this stage you may find that you encounter problems with the gelatine distorting again, and if so, you should weight it down to hold it on to the frame until the icing has dried. The weights should not be heavy, and several small ones strategically positioned are better than one large one. Leave to dry.

Arrange the flowers, leaves and dragées on top of the cakes before positioning the windows. The three windows of the top-piece are arranged by first placing the largest window so that it is parallel with the back of the cake, and setting it into a line of beading piped with a No2 nozzle and royal icing. Support it carefully until it is nearly dry, then pipe another line of beading to hold one of the side windows. This may be carefully supported against the frame of the large window while a line of beading is piped along the joint behind the frame. Place the other small window in position and strengthen the joint at the back of the frame in

the same way. Using royal icing, fix a pair of very small horseshoes to the ends of a bow of white ribbon, then secure it on to the central bar of the large window with a dot of royal icing. Place the windows on the sides of the cakes with more lines of beading, setting them so that they stand away about 6mm (¼in) from the cake. If necessary, support them with a piece of cotton wool or sponge rubber as they dry. Finally, arrange the small silver horseshoes, pastillage leaves and dragées on the cake boards between the windows.

Because the windows and frames are not very strong, do not store this cake in a sealed container as this will encourage a build-up of moisture that could make the gelatine buckle and the icing fracture. If the cake must be stored for more than a few days, it is better to make the panels from the cellophane, rather than gelatine, following the same technique. If possible, do not fix the windows to the cakes until the last moment, and keep them in a stable atmospheric environment. You can encourage the cake to remain dry by placing it in a vented box and scattering 15ml (1 tbsp) of silica gel around the base. These crystals are blue when they are dry, but will turn pink on absorbing any moisture. They can be reactivated by being dried in an oven, so don't throw them away if they change colour.

With the exception of the horseshoes, all the features of this cake are edible since there are no stamens or wires in the flowers or leaves, and no artificial materials in the other decorations.

Spring wedding

Ingredients
small long octagonal fruit cake
large long octagonal fruit cake
boiled sieved apricot jam or egg white
2.3kg (5lb) marzipan
water or alcohol
1.6kg (3lb 8oz) royal icing
800g (1lb 12oz) royal icing for piping
apple green food colouring
Cornish cream food colouring
225g (8oz) pastillage
cornflour (cornstarch)
gum arabic

Equipment
20 x 30-cm (8 x 12-in) cake board
30 x 45-cm (12 x 18-in) cake board
tracing paper
waxed paper
curved former
1 posy basket chocolate mould
No0 nozzle
No1 nozzle
No2 nozzle
No4 nozzle
vegetable parchment piping bags
3 metres (3⅜ yards) 3-mm (⅛-in)
   moss green double-sided satin ribbon
36 sugar daisies
36 sugar buttercups
8-petal medium daisy cutter
large blossom cutter
1 bundle yellow stamens
26 gauge white floristry wire
28 gauge green floristry wire
½ metre (½ yard) white tulle
½ metre (½ yard) green tulle
4 8.75-cm (3½-in) round plaster cake pillars
1 metre (1⅛ yard) 3-mm (⅛-in)
   white tubular ribbon

Number of portions
100-110

Amount of work involved
Approximately 12 hours

This two-tier cake, based on an elongated octagonal shape, brings together some of the best loved features of contemporary royal icing through a satisfying simplicity and economy of line. You should allow at least a week for the completion of this cake, as each piece must be left to dry before it is used. To save time, plan to work through the various stages in such a way that you are not held up because a particular feature of the cake has not been completed at the right moment.

After applying at least three coats of royal icing to the cakes in the usual way and leaving them to dry, prepare the templates for the runout collars and the embroidery designs, using the patterns provided. Check that the collars fit each cake top with about 12mm (½in) of support all the way round, and adjust them if necessary. If you feel confident about the sizes, you can make the collars as the cake is being iced and therefore save some time. Make the collars using flooding icing (*see page 27*) and leave to dry.

To make the half-relief baskets, make four templates of each size and place them on a flat surface, then cover each one with a small piece of waxed paper, shiny side up. Pipe over each outline with a No1 nozzle and royal icing of a normal piping consistency, ensuring that the line is unbroken. Then, using flooding icing, pipe alternate sections of the basket in the order indicated on the template, completing all the parts labelled '1' before working on those numbered '2', and finally '3'. Don't leave the icing for longer than it takes to crust over before moving on from the first group of sections to the next. Work on one basket at a time and immediately each one is complete transfer it, on its piece of waxed paper, to a curved former, such as a piece of 7.5-cm (3-in) plastic pipe split lengthways or even a baked bean can laid on its side. Leave to dry overnight into the curved shape.

The pastillage basket is made in a plastic mould. This is an inexpensive investment, as those most widely available have impressions of several shapes and sizes on a single sheet. If you are unable to obtain one, you could use a fluted fairy cake pan or the inside of an egg cup. Dust the inside of the mould with cornflour (cornstarch), then roll out a walnut-sized piece of pastillage and place it in the base of the mould, working it with your fingers until it fits the inside contours. Trim the edges with a knife and allow the pastillage to harden for an hour or two, making sure that it has been released at least once before leaving it to dry (*see page 34*). After the inside has set, turn it out of the mould so that the outside can dry. As long as the mould is clean and dry, and you work fairly quickly, you will find that this is one of the easiest processes involved in cake decorating. Because the sides of the mould are widely flared, the basket will release easily and should have a perfect finish. Make a second, smaller mould in the same way, then join the two together by their bases, with royal icing, to make a completed basket.

While the collars and baskets are setting, work on the cake itself either by applying the final coating of icing or working on the embroidery and other piping. Use a No1 nozzle to pipe the vertical

beading on the upper tier and a No2 nozzle for the
lower tier, then pipe the shell or teardrop border
around the base of each cake with a No4 nozzle.
For both cakes, the embroidery pattern is applied
with a No1 nozzle using white, green and yellow
royal icing for the various flowers, leaves and
stems. Place green ribbon around each cake and
board, and hold in place with a little royal icing.
Tie small bows and fix over the joins at the back of
each cake.

Remove the half-relief baskets from the waxed
paper and secure them to the cake by piping a line
of beading or teardrops down each side. Hold
them on to the cake for a few seconds until they
stay in place of their own accord, or support them
with a piece of cotton wool or sponge foam if
necessary. Leave the icing to set, then carefully
place a small piece of pastillage in the base of each
basket to act as a support for the ends of the daisies
and buttercups. Make the daisies with an eight-

petal medium daisy cutter, and the buttercups
with a large blossom cutter. When you have wired
them and they are dry, glaze the insides of the
buttercups with a solution of gum arabic, then set
them in position in the baskets around the cakes,
together with little fans of green tulle.

It is sound practice to leave the most delicate job
to the last whenever possible, and therefore only at
this stage should you begin to work with the icing
collars. Before removing them from their waxed
paper backing, decorate them with embroidery
and five-point lace (see page 24) and free them from
their waxed paper, then set them on the tiers,
securing them with piped beads of royal icing.

Using a No1 nozzle, pipe two parallel lines on to
each cake top, following the outline of the inside of
each collar. Finish them off in the corners with
three dots of icing pointing into the centre of the
cake. Assemble the top piece by filling the basket
with pastillage and pressing the stems of the

daisies and buttercups into it, together with some fans of green and white tulle. Make the handle of the basket by threading a wire through some tubular white ribbon, then bending it into shape and positioning it in the soft pastillage. Stick the completed basket to the surface of the top cake with a little royal icing, then arrange a few buttercups on the top of the lower cake, holding them in place with more dabs of royal icing.

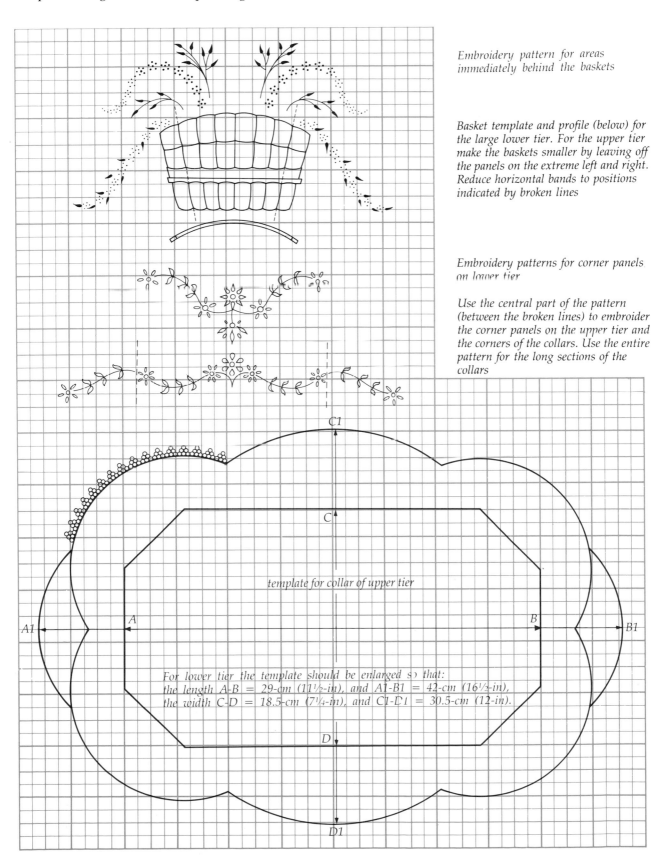

Embroidery pattern for areas immediately behind the baskets

Basket template and profile (below) for the large lower tier. For the upper tier make the baskets smaller by leaving off the panels on the extreme left and right. Reduce horizontal bands to positions indicated by broken lines

Embroidery patterns for corner panels on lower tier

Use the central part of the pattern (between the broken lines) to embroider the corner panels on the upper tier and the corners of the collars. Use the entire pattern for the long sections of the collars

template for collar of upper tier

For lower tier the template should be enlarged so that: the length A-B = 29-cm (11½-in), and A1-B1 = 42-cm (16½-in), the width C-D = 18.5-cm (7¼-in), and C1-D1 = 30.5-cm (12-in).

Nuptial bliss

Ingredients
small long octagonal fruit cake
large long octagonal fruit cake
boiled sieved apricot jam or egg white
2.3kg (5lb) marzipan
water or alcohol
3kg (6lb 8oz) sugarpaste
125g (4oz) royal icing for piping
Cornish cream food colouring
dark brown food colouring
125g (4oz) pastillage or sugarpaste
gum arabic or egg white

Equipment
20 x 30-cm (8 x 12-in) octagonal cake board
30 x 45-cm (12 x 18-in) octagon cake board
tracing paper
scriber
No0 nozzle
No1 nozzle
No2 nozzle
vegetable parchment piping bags
paintbrush
fine craft knife
pair of tweezers
4 metres (4½ yards) 3-mm (⅛-in) double-sided
 cream satin ribbon
5 metres (5½ yards) 3-mm (⅛-in) double-sided
 dark brown satin ribbon
5 metres (5½ yards) 8-mm (⅜-in) cut-edged
 cream acetate satin ribbon
6 metres (6½ yards) 8-mm (⅜-in) cut-edged
 brown acetate satin ribbon
4 20-cm (8-in) wooden skewers
4 8.75-cm (3½-in) octagonal gold plastic cake
 pillars
No4 double scalloped crimper
waxed paper
piece of card or smoother
2 gold plastic wedding rings
2 large sugar cymbidium orchids
10 sugar pulled blossom flowers
24 sugar blossom sprays
1 large orchid cutter
set of 3 blossom plunger cutters
No1 modelling tool
No5 modelling tool

Number of portions
100-110

Amount of work involved
Approximately 11 hours

One way of making a wedding cake very memorable is to incorporate the names of the bride and groom into its design. Here, they are iced on to a pastillage prayer book, but they could be piped direclty on to the top of the cake, or a set of entwined initials could be used as a decorative device around the sides of the cake. A pastillage prayer book is very useful as it can decorate all sorts of celebration cakes, especially when the reason for the celebration, or part of the ceremony itself, can be commemorated with a written record.

Cover each cake with a layer of marzipan and ivory-coloured sugarpaste in the usual way and leave to dry. Begin to make the lace (see page 46) using the template provided. You will need approximately 220 pieces for both tiers.

Make up full-sized versions of the templates provided (see page 46), then scribe the outlines on to the surface of the cakes. when scribing the patterns for the ribbon insertion, you only need to trace the two outside lines and the line where the ribbon will actually be inserted into the cake.

Using a No2 nozzle and royal icing, pipe the beading or snail trail around the base of each cake, then begin the decorations by piping the ribbon bows. This is done in sections, using an icing that is thinner than normal piping icing but about twice the thickness of flooding icing. To check its consistency, stir the icing, which has been thinned with water, until it finds its own level over about 10 seconds. Each section of the bow has a little icing piped into its centre, then using a damp paintbrush, stroke or push some of the icing out to the ends, so that it is thicker at the centre than at the ends. Leave to dry.

After completing the bows, make up a quantity of dark brown-coloured icing and, using a No0 nozzle, pipe in the embroidery patterns. The embroidery between the ribbon insertion is piped freehand. Make some ivory-coloured royal icing using Cornish cream colouring and, with a No0 nozzle, pipe a small scalloped border around both sides of the extended trail of embroidery that runs along the top of each cake and down the front and back.

To prepare the brown acetate ribbon for insertion into the icing, cut some into 12-mm (½-in) lengths and put them to one side. To insert the ribbon into the sugarpaste, make a pair of parallel slits, about 6mm (¼-in) deep, into the icing with a square-ended craft knife or special scalpel. Using a pair of tweezers, or the knife itself, guide one end of a 12-mm (½-in) length of ribbon into the first slit, and use it again to form the ribbon into a curve in order to fit the other end into the second slit. The natural springiness of the ribbon will prevent it being released. When preparing the slits for this type of decorative technique, ensure that they are evenly spaced, are parallel with one another, and

Embroidery patterns for sides

are not noticeably wider than the ribbon itself. Ribbon insertion looks very untidy if the ribbons are not level, or if the inserted loops appear to be differing widths. Continue inserting the ribbons around each cake.

To make the prayer book, roll out some brown-coloured pastillage or sugarpaste, for the cover, making it 3-mm (⅛-in) thick and about 10 x 6-cm (4 x 2½-in) in size. Use a No4 double scalloped crimper to shape and decorate the edge, then place it on a sheet of waxed paper which is in turn placed between the central pages of an open book until it has dried into a V-shape. Roll out a slightly thicker slab of ivory-coloured pastillage or sugar-paste and cut it to form a rectangle 12-mm (½-in) smaller than the cover. Carefully cut away a triangular section from the full length of each side, and use the edge of a piece of card or smoother to score parallel ridges representing the edges of the pages. Paint the centre of the brown cover with gum arabic solution or egg white, and place the ivory 'pages' in position, using the edge of a smoother or piece of card to mark the centre. When the paste has hardened, pipe an appropriate message and decoration on to the book, and secure a pair of wedding rings on the sugar with a dot of royal icing. Support the book itself on a wedge-shaped block of sugarpaste, and fill in the area beneath the covers with ribbon loops and sprays of sugar flowers.

The large pastillage cymbidium orchids, sprays of 'blossom' flowers and ribbon loops are assembled into a walnut-sized piece of sugarpaste by the set of pillars on the lower tier. Gently detach the pieces of lace from the waxed paper, then attach them to the cakes *(see page 24)*.

Centre pattern

Embroidery pattern with ribbon insertion positions

46

Moorish magic

Ingredients
15-cm (6-in) octagonal fruit cake
22.5-cm (9-in) octagonal fruit cake
30-cm (12-in) octagonal fruit cake
boiled sieved apricot jam or egg white
3.4kg (7lb 8oz) marzipan
water or alcohol
2.3kg (5lb) royal icing for coating
1.4kg (3lb) royal icing for piping
rose food colouring
cream of tartar

Equipment
20-cm (8-in) round cake board
27.5-cm (11-in) round cake board
37.5-cm (15-in) round cake board
No0 nozzle
No1 nozzle
No2 nozzle
No3 nozzle
No4 nozzle
vegetable parchment piping bags
tracing paper
waxed paper
scriber
8 8.75-cm (3½-in) plastic swan cake pillars
11.25-cm (4½-in) white plastic vase
3 medium silk roses
2 pink silk honeybells
3 white silk jasmine sprays
3 pink silk jasmine sprays
2 white silk bellflowers

Number of portions
160-170

Amount of work involved
Approximately 14 hours

A single repeated pattern of white trellis work against a rose pink background is used here to create a striking three-tier wedding cake with a Moorish appearance. The piped and flooded icing panels are slightly offset from the cake and resemble intricately carved panelling. They are surmounted by runout icing collars which reflect the form of the trellis, and are repeated in runout designs at the foot of each cake.

A cake such as this, which features a continuous facade of panels surrounding each tier, may cause you some difficulty if you are an inexperienced decorator, because the slightest irregularity in their dimensions will prevent the pieces being joined together accurately. Even if only one of them is oversized it will prove impossible to position them evenly, and if one or more of them is too small, there will be wide gaps between the panels which will have to be filled with piped icing. To reduce the risk of such problems, mark each face of each cake after it has received its final coating of royal icing so that it can be subsequently identified, and measure its precise dimensions. Then make an individual template for each of the panels. Even if the cake has been well made, you will almost certainly note some differences in size by the time your cakes have been marzipanned and iced.

Ice the cakes with three coats of pink-coloured royal icing, then ice the cake boards too, and leave to dry. The method for piping the trellis work centres for the panels is very simple. Make a template of each panel, then cover it with waxed paper and fix it in place with a dot of royal icing or masking tape on to a flat surface. Use white royal icing of a normal piping consistency, adding 1.5ml (¼ tsp) cream of tartar to every 225g (8oz) of icing to improve its working properties, although this is not essential. With a No0 nozzle, pipe all the continuous lines in one direction, then pipe those going in the opposite direction, ensuring that you achieve proper contact between the strands where they cross, and that they extend to the inside edge of the framework. Now pipe the short lengths of icing which partly bisect each square. Use the same nozzle to pipe outlines around the framework, then flood them with flooding icing (see page 26). Ensure that the ends of the trellis work are just covered, then allow the completed panels to dry out for at least 24 hours before piping the embroidery on to the top corners of each one. The eight small pieces which are used for the coronet on the top tier may be piped using the same techniques as those used for the panels. When they are dry, pipe three-point lace (see page 24) along the edges and again leave to dry. Turn the pieces over, then flood the framework, as the backs of some of the panels are visible when the pieces are standing upright on the cake.

While the side panels are drying, mark out the

pattern from the templates provided on to the cake boards, and pipe the outlines in white royal icing. Use flooding icing to fill in the area between the outline and the sides of the cakes. When these base collars are dry, pipe six-point lace around their edges.

Make the collars for the tops of the cakes (*see below*) and decorate their edges with six-point lace but do not secure them to the cake until the side panels are in position. Release the panels from their waxed paper backing and lightly fix them to each cake side in such a way as to stand slightly clear of it. To do this, pipe a pearl-sized bead of icing on to the corners of each panel with a No2 nozzle and press it gently against the cake with just enough force to squash the beads to about half their width. Do not try to force the panel hard against the cake as it may break. Put the panels in place fairly quickly as you will only have a few moments to align each one with its neighbour. Cover the join between each panel with a snail trail or beading in royal icing. If the join is poor you

may have to use a No2 nozzle for this, but if possible keep the work as delicate as possible, using a No1 or No0 nozzle. Pipe the beading along the bottom edge of each panel using a No3 or No4 nozzle, then secure each icing collar to its cake, resting it on a line of beading which has been piped along the top edge of each cake with a No3 or No4 nozzle. Add a fine line of beading below each collar where it touches the top of the panels and pipe a row of six-point lace with a No0 nozzle on the inside edge of the collar, with the points facing into the centre of the cake.

Overpipe a small octagon in the centre of the top tier, using the template provided and No1 and No0 nozzles, then position the eight small pieces of trellis for the coronet inside this piped octagon over a line of snail trail, or beading, piped with a No1 nozzle. The white plastic swan pillars and vase are widely available from cake decorators' shops, as are the artificial flowers used for the top piece. Octagonal pillars can be used instead if you want a simpler overall effect.

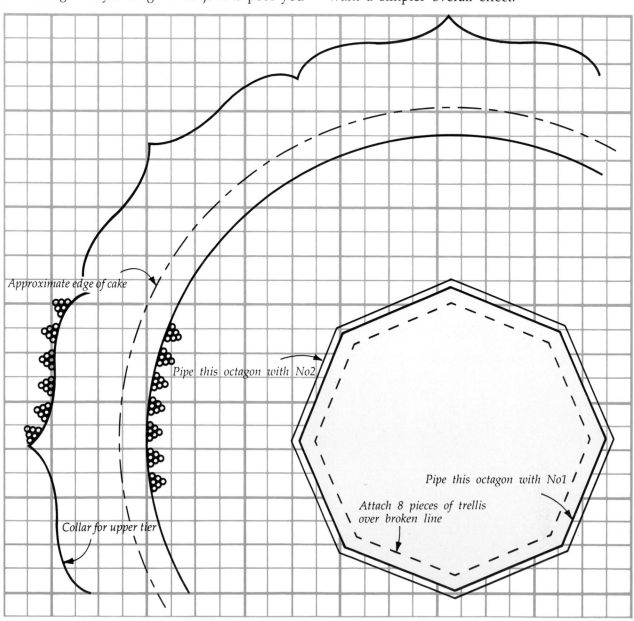

Approximate edge of cake

Pipe this octagon with No2

Collar for upper tier

Pipe this octagon with No1

Attach 8 pieces of trellis over broken line

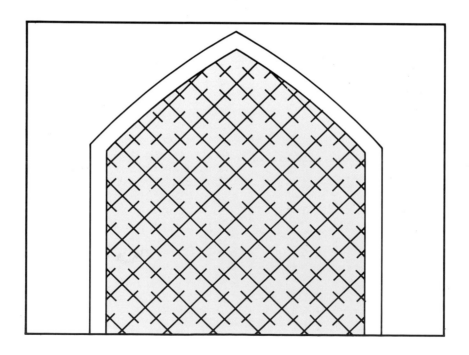

Bluebells

This unusual cake may at first glance appear complicated, but in fact it is not at all difficult to create and can be made very quickly.

Cover the cakes with a layer of marzipan and one of sugarpaste in the usual way, then place each cake on a thin cake card. Immediately trim the cake bottoms to give neat edges, then crimp them, using a No2 single scallop crimper. Secure the medium and large cakes to cake boards, 12-mm (½-in) thick and 2.5-cm (1-in) smaller than the cards, so that the bottom frill can overhang the edge of the board. This is visible in the photograph on the top tier, where the lowest frill has been removed. Leave the cakes for at least 24 hours to allow the sugarpaste to harden.

Before applying the frills each cake must be accurately marked out into five sections. The simplest way to do this is to draw a circle, about 25-cm (10-in) in diameter, then draw a straight line from the centre point to the edge of the circle. From this starting point, and using a protractor, mark off a position giving an angle of 72°, then draw another line from the centre point to the edge of the circle. Turn the paper and repeat the process

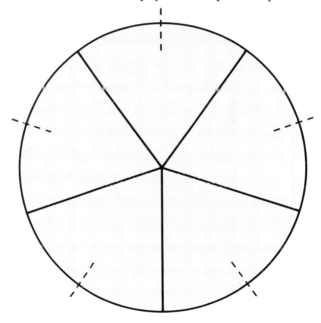

three more times, each time using the new line as the starting point. Next, stand each cake in turn on the centre of the circle and use the guidelines to mark the five segments on the sugarpaste and also to mark the centres of each segment while the cake is in position on the paper.

Make full-size templates from the patterns provided and scribe a curved triangle on to each of the segments. Use the convex side as the base with the apex as the topmost point for the frilled icing. Before beginning the next stage, note that you will require six rows of frills on the lower and middle tiers, and five on the top tier although, in each case, only the two lowest rows of frills extend all the way round the cakes.

To make the frills, roll out a piece of sugarpaste until it is extremely thin and almost transparent. Use a ratio of up to two parts sugarpaste to one part pastillage if you want the frills to be very stiff. Work on one cake at a time, wrapping the rest of the sugarpaste in a plastic bag, then placing it in an air-tight container to prevent it drying out. Cut a circle out of the paste about 10-cm (4-in) in diameter, using either a scalloped or plain round cutter, then cut out another circle from the centre of the original circle. The width of the ring of remaining sugarpaste will become the width of the frill. Place the ring of paste on a work surface liberally dusted with cornflour (cornstarch), then hold a wooden cocktail stick (wooden toothpick) at right angles to the sugarpaste, with about 12-mm (½-in) of one end resting on the paste. Using your index finger, rotate or roll the stick steadily against the icing, keeping your finger about 6-mm (¼-in) away from the edge of the paste. This squeezes and stretches it and, as the cocktail stick rolls along the icing, it will pucker up and form the fluted frill. When the ring has been made into a complete frill, cut along one side to open it out. With a wet paintbrush, paint a line of water along the bottom of the cake and attach the top of the frill to the dampened area. Support the frill across the length of your hand and feed it on to the cake, always pressing the top edge gently into place with the thumb or fingertips of your free hand. Alternatively you can use the rounded end of a piece of 6-mm (¼-in) dowelling or a dogbone modelling tool. Ensure that the lower frill is positioned so it just obscures the crimping at the base of the cake.

Make and position the next row of frills in the same way, ensuring that it half-covers the one beneath it. Position the subsequent rows of frills within the scribed triangles. When all five segments are filled, apply a final band of frills along the edge of each segment.

Prepare three sizes of template, from those provided, to make the petals that drape across the upper part of each cake. Colour about 700g (1½lb) of sugarpaste with cornflower blue food colouring, then roll out half of it to a thickness of 6-mm (¼-in) and cut out five petals. Cover these with a plastic bag or piece of polythene and store the remaining

sugarpaste as before until needed. Taking each petal in turn, crimp around the edges with a No2 single scallop crimper, then turn the petal over and moisten the upper half with a little water. Drape the petal over the side of the cake so that the upper ends rest over the areas of smooth sugarpaste not decorated with frills, and curl up the ends and support them on cotton wool until they have hardened. Once all five petals are in position, conceal the point at which they meet by securing a small circle of sugarpaste, about 12-mm (½-in) in diameter, to the top of the cake with a little water, then hang chains of silk flowers from it. Then place a larger silk flower on the central point where the stems and strands meet.

The triangular templates when cut out, may be used according to their size, to mark out the areas which will be decorated with frills on each of the three sizes of cake

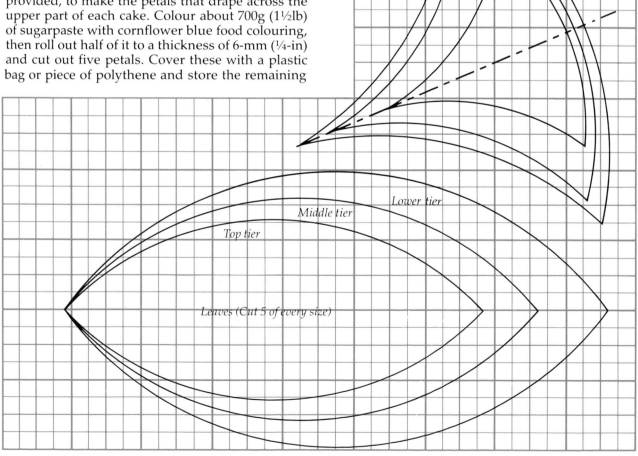

Lower tier

Middle tier

Top tier

Leaves (Cut 5 of every size)

Congratulations!

Ingredients
25-cm (10-in) bell-shaped fruit cake
boiled sieved apricot jam or egg white
1.1kg (2½lb) marzipan
water or alcohol
550g (1¼lb) white royal icing
125g (4oz) royal icing for piping

Equipment
30-cm (12-in) bell-shaped cake board
plastic or metal scraper with serrated edge
2 metres (2⅛ yards) 12-mm (½-in)
  silver banding
No1 nozzle
No44 nozzle
vegetable parchment piping bags
1 large sugar filigree ring
2 metres (2⅛ yards) blue decorette ribbon
3 large blue wafer roses
6 small blue wafer roses
9 green wafer leaves
1 'Congratulations' motto
6 small silver horseshoes

Number of portions
35-40

Amount of work involved
Approximately 2½ hours

This bell-shaped cake is an unusual choice for a small wedding, but it can look very effective. Although it is shown here as a single cake, it looks equally attractive if paired with an identical cake and positioned on a large cake board so that the upper parts of each bell are nearly touching.

Cover the cake with a layer of marzipan and three coats of royal icing in the usual way, then leave to dry. Now apply a fourth layer of royal icing to the sides of the cake, and create the ridged effect by combing the wet icing with a plastic or metal scraper with a serrated edge. The scraper removes some of the icing and allows the remainder to pass through the gaps between the teeth, leaving an evenly dispersed pattern of horizontal bands. The scraper used for this cake has regular V-shaped teeth, but there are many other patterns available, such as semi-circular or square-cut serrations. Leave the icing until dry, then wrap the silver banding around the outside of the cake board, holding it in place with dabs of royal icing.

Fit a piping bag with a No44 nozzle and fill with white royal icing, then pipe a row of shells along the top and bottom edges of the cake. Using a No1 nozzle, pipe small dots between the shells. Fix a sugar filigree ring *(see pages 67-68)* to the curved end of the bell, using tiny dabs of royal icing to hold it in place. This represents the mounting loop at the top of church bells. Leave to dry. Wrap the blue ribbon around the side of the cake, holding it in place with dots of royal icing. Join the two ends of the ribbon at the centre front of the cake, secure with more royal icing and leave to dry. Using icing, fix a large wafer rose and three wafer leaves over the join in the ribbon to represent the bell's clapper. On top of the cake, arrange the remaining wafer roses, and their leaves, in an attractive spray pattern, and hold in place with tiny dots of royal icing. Fix the 'Congratulations' motto to the top of the cake, and stick the silver horseshoes to the ribbon around the side of the cake, at regular intervals, using more small dots of icing.

Bellissima

Ingredients
fruit cake mixture baked in a large
 bell-shaped 'tiffin' tin pan
boiled sieved apricot jam or egg white
2.3kg (5lb) marzipan
water or alcohol
2.8kg (6lb) sugarpaste
225g (8oz) royal icing for piping
moss green food colouring
rose pink food colouring
fuchsia pink petal dust
pink lustre colour

Equipment
30 x 45-cm (12 x 18-in) cake board
brown paper
No0 nozzle
No1 nozzle
No42 nozzle
vegetable parchment piping bags
tracing paper
scriber
5metres (5½ yards) 3-mm (⅛-in) double-sided
 white satin ribbon
5 metres (5½ yards) 8-mm (⅜-in) white acetate
 satin ribbon
6 pastillage carnations
10 pastillage sweet peas
8 pastillage sweet pea buds
carnation cutter
sweet pea cutter
set of blossom plunger cutters
11 small blossom sprays
1 bundle pink stamens
1 bundle white stamens
white 26 gauge floristry wire

Number of portions
50

Amount of work involved
Approximately 6½ hours

This double bell cake is actually a single cake baked in a large bell-shaped 'tiffin' tin (pan), and then sliced in half through the centre. In order to bake this cake successfully, long slow cooking is vital. Otherwise, owing to its shape, the narrow end will be overcooked while the thicker end may be undercooked. It is a good idea to stand the narrow end of the tin in a small round tin for extra insulation and also to stop the cake toppling over. As it is an unusual shape, it is not easy to line the tin completely with paper. Instead, cut out a 12.5-

cm (5-in) circle of brown paper, then make cuts at intervals of about 5-cm (2-in) around the circumference to converge near the centre so that when the paper is pushed into position, the segments overlap one another and the resulting cone fits the inside contours of the tin. Coat the inside of the tin with a layer of fat and flour, then insert the circle of brown paper before filling it with the cake mixture. The cake must be released from the tin while it is still hot.

Whenever you have to cut a cake that contains a high proportion of dried fruit or nuts, it is best to allow the cake to mature for two to three weeks first to stop the mixture crumbling too much. It is also helpful to use a really sharp knife with a serrrated cutting edge. Having cut the cake in half, coat each piece with a layer of marzipan and then one of sugarpaste, moulding the icing on the broad ends of the half bells until it is as flat as possible. To prevent any visible finger-prints, lift each cake on to the cake board with a large spatula or smoother, then arrange them close together. With a No42 nozzle pipe a small shell border around each cake. If the bells touch at the top, pipe the shells as far round as possible.

Using the templates provided, transfer the outlines of the embroidery on to the cakes, repeating the top pattern four times on each bell. Then pipe in the embroidery with a No0 nozzle and pink and white royal icing. With a No1 nozzle, pipe tiny scallops just beneath the rim of each bell and leave

to dry. Decorate the point where the top of the bells meet, and the areas where the clappers would be, with arrangements of ribbons and sugar flowers, the stems of which have been pressed into separate pads of sugarpaste. Make at least 80 pieces of the lacework, using the template provided, and leave to dry, then attach the pieces to the rims of the bells *(see page 24)*.

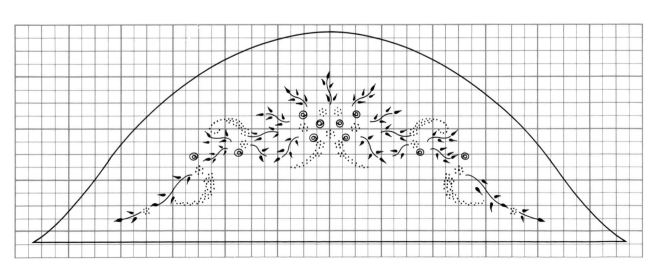

Summer roses

Ingredients
small oval fruit cake
medium oval fruit cake
large oval fruit cake
boiled sieved apricot jam or egg white
2.8kg (6lb) marzipan
water or alcohol
3.1kg (6lb 10oz) sugarpaste
50g (2oz) royal icing for piping
50g (2oz) pastillage
burgundy food colouring
rose food colouring
plum dusting colour
gum arabic

Equipment
25-cm (10-in) oval cake board
30-cm (12-in) oval cake board
40-cm (16-in) oval cake board
3 scalloped crimpers, one of each size
sheet of thin card
tracing paper
scriber
No1 nozzle
vegetable parchment piping bags
small and medium blossom plunger cutters
small, medium and large heart-shaped
    plunger cutters
3 7.5-cm (3-in) white octagonal cake pillars
3 8.75-cm (3½-in) white octagonal cake pillars
5 metres (5½ yards) 3-mm (⅛-in)
    double-sided burgundy satin ribbon
2½ metres (2¾ yards) 3-mm (⅛-in)
    double-sided pink satin ribbon
3 metres (3⅜ yards) 8-mm (⅜-in)
    white acetate satin ribbon
4 sugar rosebuds
5 white sugar blossom sprays
    with pink stamens
3 white sugar blossom sprays
    with pearl stamens

Number of portions
170-180

Amount of work involved
Approximately 6 hours

Although this cake has three tiers and is an unusual shape, it is surprisingly simple. Since it has hardly any piping it is ideal for beginners. The cakes are covered with sugarpaste, which must be of a high quality and free from gritty lumps, so that it will remain flexible and won't crack while it is being moulded. It must also remain workable and soft enough to accept the design that is impressed into the sides of the cakes.

Cover the cakes with marzipan, then position each one on its board and cover both the board and the cake with sugarpaste, making sure it doesn't crack. Avoid any interruptions or the sugarpaste may dry out before you finish work. Smooth the sugarpaste down over each cake, across each board and down over its sides, then trim the edge of the sugarpaste with scallop-shaped crimpers to create a fluted effect against the sides of the board. You can use different sizes of crimper to create additional interest.

The pattern is applied to the sides of the cakes by marking the sugarpaste with a stencil made from a sheet of thin card. Cut it to the correct size, then gently press it against the sugarpaste to provide a bare outline. This is then accentuated with the scalloped crimpers. Using the three sizes of plain-ended, not serrated, crimpers, press them gently against the icing but don't penetrate it fully, As they begin to bite, withdraw them slightly and then release the pressure on the jaws as they are withdrawn completely. If they seem to stick and drag at the icing, dip the jaws into a little icing (confectioner's) sugar. Follow the pattern around the cake, working continuously so the sugarpaste will not dry out before you have finished.

With an oval template, mark a line where the sugarpaste rim is to be positioned on the top of each cake, and dampen the line with water. Roll out a sausage of sugarpaste to about the diameter of a pencil and press it gently on to the dampened sugarpaste. Taking care only to partially close the jaws of the crimpers, form the oval into scalloped curves.

Trace over the outlines for the simple icing embroidery to make a template, then use it to mark the sides of each cake. Pipe the stems and leaves in plain white royal icing, and the forget-me-not flowers in plum-coloured royal icing, both with a No1 nozzle. To make the other flowers for the sides of the cakes, roll out some plum-coloured pastillage, then stamp out flowers with small, medium and large blossom cutters. To make the pink flowers on the sides of each cake, roll out some pink-coloured pastillage, then stamp out heart shapes using the small, medium and large cutters. Each flower is made from five hearts, which are immediately glued to the cake with a mixture of one part gum arabic to three parts water. Pipe a dot of plum-coloured royal icing into

the centre of each flower. Dust a narrow line of plum dusting colour around the scalloped edge of each board, then brush it off to create a gently diffused effect. Then secure the plum-coloured flowers between the scallops around the sides of each board with a dot of royal icing.

Wrap burgundy ribbon around each cake, securing it with a dot of royal icing. Cover the join with a small bow. The top cake tier is decorated with a mixture of moulded sugar roses and sprays of blossom flowers, some of which have been tinted with plum dusting colour. Curl toning pink- and plum-coloured florist's ribbons by running a blunt knife or the edge of a pair of scissors along their length, then arrange them amongst the flowers on the top tier to give extra height and fullness to the arrangement. Satin ribbon will not curl, so make up a series of ribbon loops and assemble with the sugar flowers into a walnut-sized piece of sugar-paste.

Arrows show the position of sugar flowers between the piped embroidery, located above the small tier crimper pattern. The larger pattern for the lower tier is indicated below it and the embroidery is the same.

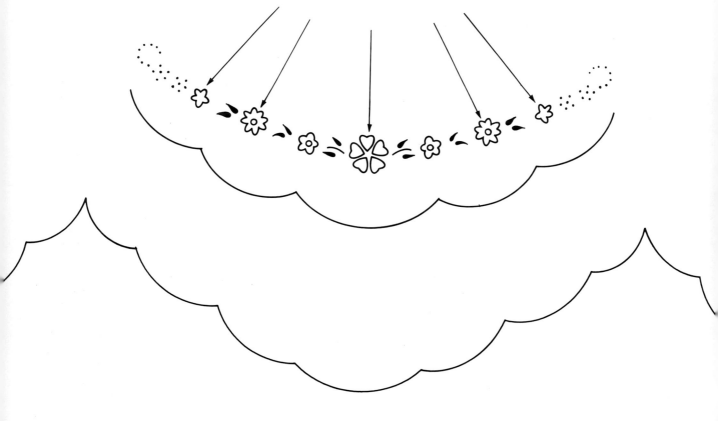

Scandinavian celebration

Ingredients
20-cm (8-in) oval fruit cake
32.5-cm (13-in) oval fruit cake
boiled sieved apricot jam or egg white
2.2kg (4lb 8oz) marzipan
water or alcohol
1.9kg (4lb 4oz) royal icing
125g (4oz) royal icing for piping
900g (2lb) pastillage or gum paste
cornflour (cornstarch)
apple green food colouring
Christmas red food colouring

Equipment
25-cm (10-in) oval cake board
40-cm (16-in) oval cake board
tracing paper
single scallop mini crimper
medium heart-shaped plunger cutter
small heart-shaped plunger cutter
scriber
No0 nozzle
No1 nozzle
No2 nozzle
No3 nozzle
No4 nozzle
vegetable parchment piping bags
5 metres (5½ yards) green ribbon
2 large red silk roses
10 large green silk leaves
3 10-cm (4-in) plaster cake pillars

Number of portions
100-105

Amount of work involved
Approximately 8 hours

The bright and cheerful designs embroidered in red- and green-coloured royal icing bear a resemblance to the Scandinavian style of design known as Tole painting. The arrangement of wafer-thin double collars on this oval cake is very unusual since they are very delicate, but are made of pastillage or gum paste rather than royal icing.

Cover the two cakes with marzipan and royal icing in the usual way, coat the cake boards with royal icing, and leave to dry. Then make the four collars (*see page 63*), as they can be hardening while you decorate the rest of the cake. Each pair of collars has the same overall shape except that the heart-shaped flower pattern is not cut out of the lower collar in each set. Leave the pastillage to stand for at least 24 hours before using, as this makes it more flexible and elastic, and you can roll it out thinly with less danger of it cracking. Make the templates from the pattern provided. Take about half the mixture (wrap the remainder in a plastic bag, then place in an air-tight container) and roll out on a board dusted with cornflour (cornstarch). To ensure that it does not stick to the board as it becomes progressively thinner, lift it at intervals and sprinkle more cornflour beneath it, working quickly to prevent the paste drying out. Roll it out until it is abour 2-mm (¹/₁₂-in) thick, then place a template on top of the paste and cut around it with a sharp knife. Cut out the oval section in the middle, placing all the offcuts back in the bag with the rest of the pastillage. If you wish to crimp around the edges of the collar, cover the collar with a piece of plastic wrap and only expose the area of pastillage on which you are working. With a single scallop mini crimper, crimp both the inside and outside of the collar, then cut out the heart-shaped sections on each quarter of the upper collar with medium and small heart-shaped plunger cutters. Replace the template to check that you have not accidentally stretched the pastillage out of shape. If so, carefully ease it back with your hand until the correct shape is regained. Work on each of the collars in the same way, but only cut out the heart-shapes on the upper two collars.

It is most important to allow large pieces of pastillage to dry evenly on both sides, and therefore the collars should be turned over every two or three hours at first. Take care not to break them, so begin by drying each one on its own board and place another board over the pastillage when you need to turn it. Turn over both boards, with the collar sandwiched between the two, and remove the upper board, thus exposing to the air what was previously the under surface of the pastillage. Leave the collars to dry completely for at least 48 hours. In the meantime, prepare the collar supports by rolling out long sausage-shaped pieces of pastillage to the circumference of each inside collar, then flatten them so they can be cut into two strips 2.5-cm (1-in) wide. Form each strip into an oval and stand it on one edge to dry.

Using the templates provided, trace the embroidery on to the sides of the two cakes, then scribe the outlines of the collars on to each cake board. Pipe a line of beading or shells around the bottom of each cake, using a No3 or No4 nozzle and white royal icing. With a No1 nozzle and white royal icing, pipe over the outlines of the collars on the boards. If you wish, you can use a No2 nozzle for this linework, then overpipe the lines with a No1 nozzle before finishing the piped design with a continuous scallop pattern using a No0 nozzle.

Pipe the embroidery patterns with red- and green-coloured royal icing and a No0 nozzle.

Alternatively, you can use red and green edible food colouring pens to draw the embroidery on to the sides of the cakes, in which case the designs could be highly intricate.

When the pastillage is dry, scribe the embroidery designs on to the two upper collars and pipe on, or draw on, the embroidery patterns. Wrap green ribbon around the lower portion of each cake and secure with dabs of royal icing. Position the lower collars on the two cakes, using piped

lines of beading to hold them in place, then attach the collar supports in the same way. Leave to set in position. Pipe lines of beading around the tops of the two collar supports and carefully place the upper collars in position. Leave to dry, then wrap ribbon around each collar support, holding it in place with dabs of royal icing. Arrange the silk flowers and leaves in the wells formed at the centre of each cake.

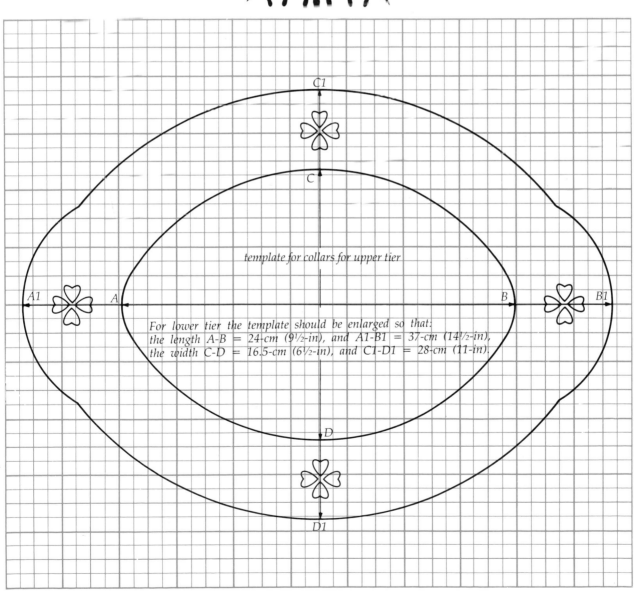

template for collars for upper tier

For lower tier the template should be enlarged so that:
the length A-B = 24-cm (9½-in), and A1-B1 = 37-cm (14½-in),
the width C-D = 16.5-cm (6½-in), and C1-D1 = 28-cm (11-in).

Rustic wedding

Ingredients
large oval fruit cake
boiled sieved apricot jam or egg white
1.4kg (3lb) marzipan
water or alcohol
1.4kg (3lb) sugarpaste
350g (12oz) royal icing for piping
apple green food colouring
black food colouring
Christmas red food colouring
Cornish cream food colouring
moss green food colouring
50g (2oz) piping gel

Equipment
40-cm (16-in) oval cake board
No4 scallop crimper
crescent-shaped embossing tool
tracing paper
scriber
No3 sable paintbrushes
No0 nozzle
No1 nozzle
No2 nozzle
vegetable parchment piping bags
2 gold plastic wedding rings
pack of edible gold leaf or gold flake
5 red sugar poppies
small bundle black stamens

Number of portions
80-85

Amount of work involved
Approximately 5 hours

Decorated with corn poppies and ears of wheat encircled by a pair of gold wedding rings, this cake is perfect for a late summer country wedding.

Colour the sugarpaste with a little Cornish cream colouring the day before you intend to ice the cake. In the meantime, marzipan the cake. When the sugarpaste is ready, first use it to cover the board, trimming the edge with a sharp knife. Impress scallops around the edge with a No4 crimper, then press a crescent-shaped embossing tool against the sugarpaste to create a pattern above the crimped scallops. Cover the cake in the normal way, making sure it has a clean edge. Place it in the centre of the cake board and leave for at least 48 hours, to allow the sugarpaste to harden before marking out the patterns for the sprays of poppies and ears of wheat.

Make templates of the embroidery designs from the patterns provided, then scribe them on to the sides and top of the cake. Create the flowers on the sides of the cake, and the background leaves and daisies on the top, with brush embroidery *(see page 66)*. Then pipe the half-relief ears of wheat directly on to the sides and top of the cake using a No1 nozzle for the stems and a No2 nozzle for the wheat itself, and royal icing tinted with Cornish cream colouring to match the sugarpaste. Pipe the stems first, then the two rows of offset pointed beads, or teardrops, of icing to represent the grains arranged in lines so that the bulbous end of each bead is only just touching its opposite neighbour. Work all the way round the cake piping these first two rows, then, when they are dry, pipe another row down the centre, between the two earlier rows, and finish the line with a grain piped directly on to the icing. Six to eight grains are sufficient for each row.

The miniature wheatsheaf, around which the wedding rings are placed, is prepared in much the same way, except that the beads, or grains, of icing are piped on to long stalks or thin-covered wire which are laid on a sheet of waxed paper. When the first three rows of grains are dry, carefully lift the whole stalk off the paper, turn it over and then repeat the process on the back, so that when each one is finished and dried it is three-dimensional, with the grains of wheat completely covering the wire. Pipe about twelve ears of wheat and leave to dry, then thread them through the two gold rings, sticking them into position with a small dot of royal icing.

To make the gold ribbon that is used to tie the bunch of flowers together on top of the cake, flood Cornish cream-coloured royal icing in sections on to the top of the cake, working without piped outlines. Leave to harden before gilding it with gold leaf or gold flake. You may find this difficult if you are an inexperienced decorator, as the material is so fine that it can tear very easily, may float

about and usually sticks wherever it lands. If you do decide to gild the icing, pick the gold from its vial with the tip of a very soft paintbrush and smoothly transfer it to the area to be treated. Moisten the surface of the icing very carefully with a little water, or with piping gel placed on a second paintbrush, and touch the dry gilding brush against it. The gold will instantly adhere to the dampened area. If any of the gold overlaps the intended area, pick it off with a fine scalpel. Then burnish the surface by brushing the gold in one direction with a gentle stroking motion.

Pipe a tiny trail of beading around the bottom of the cake, using a No0 nozzle and cream-coloured royal icing, and a continuous herringbone band of teardrops to represent wheat grains around the sides of the cake using a No2 nozzle. Fix the sugar poppies to the embroidery on the top of the cake.

Togetherness

This is a difficult cake to make, but the results are well worth the effort involved! When piping such large and delicate filigree pieces as these, they can often break, caused by a patch of weak or poor-quality royal icing. Each professional cake decorator has their own method of counteracting this problem — some insist on using natural aged egg whites in their mixture, some use powdered egg albumen since the ratio of albumen can be easily increased to give a stronger mix, while others add a pinch of gum tragacanth to each 450g (1lb) of icing. However, we have found that adding a pinch of cream of tartar to each 450g (1lb) of royal icing and then letting the mixture stand for 24 hours, works for us. Try each of these suggestions until you find the one that suits you best.

Bake the cakes in their spherical tins (pans), then cover with marzipan and sugarpaste and leave to harden (*see page 70*). Cover the boards with sugarpaste, then cut out scallops around the edges with the crimper. Position the cakes in the centre of each board. Because the cakes may not be exactly the same size as these designs once they have been covered, cut out the outline of the templates from a piece of stiff card and then physically match them up to the curvature of your covered cakes. If any gaps or high points show up between the templates and the icing, adjust the curved edge until it fits exactly. If you have to make individual templates, mark each one so that you will know where to position it when the icing is completed.

Transfer the design on to tracing paper and place it on a flat white background, then cover it with a thin clear acrylic sheet, or piece of glass, about 3-mm (⅛-in) thick. On top of this place a sheet of fairly heavy gauge polythene or PVC film and secure each corner with masking tape. Work on one piece of filigree at a time. Pipe in the faces of the bride and groom with a No00 nozzle, then change to a No0 nozzle and pipe in the finer details of the suit and dress, followed by the principal lines, which are marked in thick ink on the template and piped with a No0 or No1 nozzle. Ensure that all the piping is neat and the linework evenly spaced. Where lines meet, ensure that they really do meet and do not stop short of one another. Use a moist paintbrush to wipe away any overlapping filigree or untidy work.

When each filigree piece is completed, allow it to dry for at least 24 hours, then carefully remove the plastic film from the board without bending it. Place a piece of foam sponge rubber, slightly larger than the pattern, on the working surface and, keeping the film taut, turn it over and position it over the foam with the filmside uppermost. Peel the foam away from the filigree, which will be left resting upside down on the foam. Wipe the piece of film clean and, making sure it is completely dry, slide it back under the piece of filigree. This will

enable you to pick up the filigree again when you have finished piping. Now pipe around the outline and principal curves of the pattern again, using a No0 or No1 nozzle, and allow the filigree to dry for a further 24 hours.

While the filigree pieces are drying, pipe the brush embroidery (*see page 66*) on to the sides of the cakes and the boards, using a No1 nozzle and white royal icing, having first scribed it on to the sugarpaste through a template. To pipe the filigree leaves, make templates from the pattern provided and pipe over the outlines (*see page 67*), then leave to dry in a former. Position these on top of the cakes with royal icing before attaching the side pieces, because if you drop one you are less likely to knock one of the filigree wing sections. Be very careful when placing the final piece in position as there is very little room in which to work.

To successfully secure a large piece of filigree in position, it is important to think ahead and assemble all the equipment you may need, especially foam supports before starting work. Using a No1 nozzle and white royal icing, pipe a vertical line, or a fine line of beading, down the length of the cake where the filigree is to be positioned. Check this first with the cardboard template, then gently pick up the filigree, holding a strengthened part such as the bouquet of flowers, and set it in place holding it gently but firmly against the cake for a few seconds, with the filigree extending at right angles to its surface. If the piping leans to one side, support it with small wedges of foam rubber or cotton wool. When the filigree piece is stable, strengthen the join by piping a fine snail trail or line of beading along the back and front of the join, then attach the second and subsequent pieces.

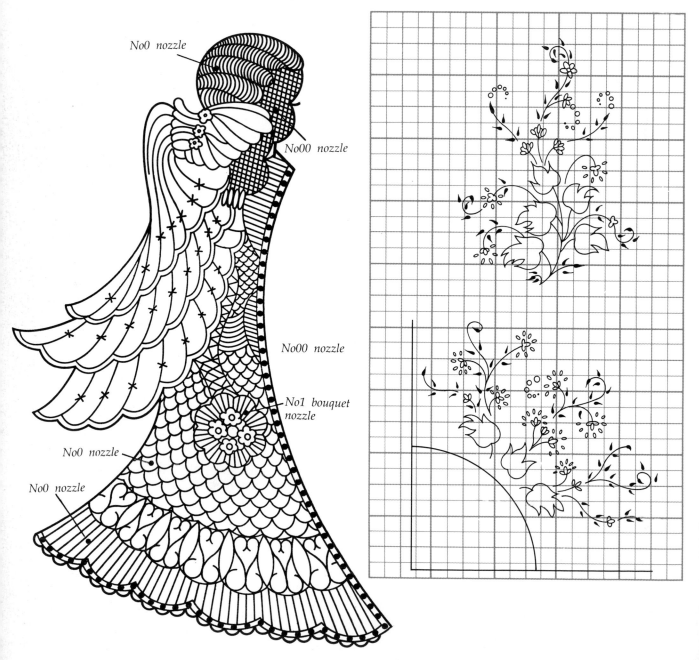

No0 nozzle

No00 nozzle

No00 nozzle

No1 bouquet nozzle

No0 nozzle

No0 nozzle

Perfect posy

Ingredients
1.9kg (4lb 6oz) Madeira or fruit cake mixture
boiled sieved apricot jam or egg white
700g (1lb 8oz) marzipan
water or alcohol
1.1kg (2lb 8oz) sugarpaste
50g (2oz) royal icing for piping
lemon yellow food colouring
violet food colouring

Equipment
large spherical cake tin (pan)
10-cm (4-in) cake card
25-cm (10-in) round cake board
1 metre (1⅛ yards) lacelon frill
½ metre (½ yard) yellow decorette ribbon
120 2.5-cm (1-in) silk buttercups or daisies
waxed paper
tracing paper
No1 nozzle
vegetable parchment piping bag
wooden cocktail sticks (wooden toothpicks)

Number of portions
30

Amount of work involved
Approximately 3 hours

This attractive, but distinctly unusual, cake could almost be more of a table decoration than a true wedding cake. If decorated with silk flowers that match those carried by the bride or bridesmaids, it would make a perfect present for some honoured guests, such as the parents of the bride.

The cake can either be a Madeira or a fruit cake mixture, and is baked in a spherical tin (pan) of the type originally intended for traditional Christmas puddings. The tin consists of two halves, one of which is completely filled with the cake mixture, and then clamped to its partner, which is half-filled and secured on a simple stand. There is usually a hole in the top of the upper half through which moisture is released as the cake is cooked and the mixture expands to fill the void. When the cake is ready it must be released from the tin while it is still hot, for this tin cannot be lined with paper. Instead the interior should be brushed with fat and dusted with flour, or sprayed with a non-stick release medium specially formulated for baking.

When the cake has cooled, fill any gaps or irregularities in the surface of the cake with pieces of marzipan. If the cake has been standing on a flat surface for more than a few hours, it will have developed a flat area about 10-cm (4-in) across, which must be disguised with a piece of marzipan, cut to the same shape, and stuck over the cake with a little apricot jam or egg white. Then roll out a large piece of marzipan into a circular shape, the diameter of which is roughly equivalent to the circumference of the cake less the piece of marzipan already attached. Measure the cake tin to determine the approximate size. Cover the exposed surface of the cake with jam or egg white, then drape the marzipan over it, smoothing it down and compressing it towards the base where the marzipan is already in position. Mould it into shape by smoothing and warming it with the palms of your hands until it follows the ball shape, then trim off any excess pieces. The easiest way to do this is to turn the cake upside down and trim off any surplus, making sure there is a good join to the original marzipan circle. Leave to harden for at least 24 hours.

Repeat this technique using sugarpaste, but this time spreading the marzipan with a little alcohol or water first. Place the cake on a thin piece of cake card, 10-cm (4-in) in diameter. Begin decorating the cake from the base, securing each flower and leaf to the cake with tiny beads of royal icing. Do not stick any wires into the sugarpaste if the cake is to be eaten. When you have completed the first two rows, place the cake on a piece of lacelon frill and position it on the cake board. Complete the decoration by covering the entire cake with flowers and leaves. Fix a loop of ribbon to the top of the cake to suggest a handle.

To make the butterflies or bees, flood them on to

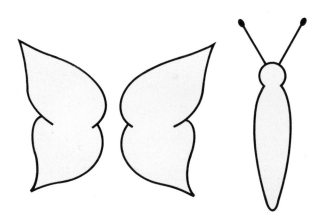

70

waxed paper placed over templates traced from the patterns provided *(see left)*. To thicken the bodies of the butterfly or bumble bee, use a No1 nozzle and pipe a second coating of icing on the undersides, once they have been removed from the paper. Make the bodies from yellow- or brown-coloured icing and paint on their markings with food colouring, or draw them on with edible food colouring pens. Insert stamens into the icing while it is still wet to represent the antennae, and leave to dry. The insects can be stuck directly on to the cake with royal icing, or mounted on to a piece of wire or the tip of a wooden cocktail stick (wooden toothpick). To cut the cake, slice it in half, then remove it from its board, place it on its flat side and cut it as though it were a loaf of bread.

Forget-me-not

Ingredients
small petal-shaped fruit cake
large petal-shaped fruit cake
boiled sieved apricot jam or egg white
1.8kg (3lb 14oz) marzipan
water or alcohol
1.85kg (4lb 2oz) royal icing
125g (4oz) royal icing for piping
50g (2oz) pastillage
apple green food colouring
cornflower blue food colouring
ice blue food colouring
violet food colouring

Equipment
25-cm (10-in) round cake board
40-cm (16-in) round cake board
silver banding
No1 nozzle
No2 nozzle
No44 nozzle
vegetable parchment piping bags
120 sugar blossoms in shades of blue and violet
set of 3 blossom plunger cutters
4 8.75-cm (3½-in) round plaster cake pillars
11.25-cm (4½-in) blue plastic vase
12 blue silk verbena sprays
12 mauve silk verbena sprays
4 mauve silk lily of the valley garlands

Number of portions
100-105

Amount of work involved
Approximately 4½ hours

Although this cake looks quite straightforward and simple, finishing it well can be quite a demanding task! It is the very simplicity of its design that means any imperfections in the royal icing will be very noticeable.

Because of the petal shape of the cakes, it is essential that you carefully control the side-scraper when working in the concave sections between each petal or bulge. It will help to place the cake on a smooth-running turntable and you may also find it an advantage to place a damp flannel or cloth between the board and the turntable to stop the cake sliding about. By resting the elbow of your 'icing arm' comfortably on the work surface beside the turntable, you will be able to control the movement of your forearm and wrist, following the alternating concave and convex curves as the slowly rotating cake passes beneath the blade of the scraper.

Leave each coat of icing to dry for at least 12 hours before applying the next, and if necessary smooth the penultimate coat with fine glasspaper before applying the final very thin layer of icing. If the royal icing is of the correct consistency, and every coat is built up carefully and evenly, there should never be any need to use the glasspaper. When completed, the thickness of the icing across the top and sides of the cake should be approximately 6-mm (¼-in) thick. At the same time as coating the cakes, coat each board with three layers of royal icing and trim with silver banding when dry. Pipe a band of beading, using a No2 nozzle, around the edge of each board.

With a No44 nozzle and white royal icing, pipe a shell border around the top and bottom of each cake, then, using a No1 nozzle, pipe small drop loops below each of the top edging shells and tiny 'seed pearls' between the shells on the cake boards. Leave to dry.

To make the forget-me-nots, colour the pastillage in three harmonious colours to match the ribbons and silk flowers of the top piece. Roll the paste out in a thin sheet, then stamp the forget-me-nots out with flower cutters and cup them by pressing their centres into a piece of soft sponge or foam rubber before they have a chance to dry. Fix them to the sides of the cakes with small dabs of royal icing, which can also be used to decorate their centres, arranging them as garlands around the cakes. Give these garlands a slight lift by decorating the area between each flower with a minute pattern of green-coloured royal icing piped, with a No1 nozzle, as teardrops to suggest leaves. Arrange small posies of flowers on the surface of each cake at the concave points of the petals, then place more flowers on the cake boards. Fill the vase with silk flowers and place in the centre of the top tier when the cake is finally assembled.

The secret of a well-finished royal icing surface lies less with a final flourish with a bowl full of icing and an icing rule, than with a painstaking attention to detail in preparing the foundation covering of marzipan. It is at this stage when any flaws in the cake itself must be eliminated. Then, when the first of the three coats of icing is applied, there will be no bumps or projections to impede its flow under the edge of a scraper or icing rule.

Roses all the way

Ingredients
25-cm (10-in) petal-shaped fruit cake
boiled sieved apricot jam or egg white
700g (1½lb) marzipan
water or alcohol
950g (2lb 2oz) sugarpaste
125g (4oz) royal icing for piping
apple green food colouring
moss green food colouring
moss green dusting colour for flowers
yellow dusting colour for flowers
125g (4oz) pastillage (optional)

Equipment
37.5-cm (15-in) petal-shaped cake board
1 sheet silver patterned gift wrapping paper
spray adhesive
tracing paper
scriber
No0 nozzle
No1 nozzle
vegetable parchment piping bags
fine paintbrush
ball modelling tool
No1 dogbone modelling tool
star/cone modelling tool
7 large white sugar roses
5 medium white sugar roses
3 small white sugar roses
12 very small white sugar roses
6 white sugar rose buds
20 sugar rose leaves of various sizes
18 sugar stephanotis flowers
6 sugar blossoms
9 metres (10 yards) 3-mm (⅛-in)
  double-sided moss green satin ribbon
2 metres (2¼ yards) 3-mm (⅛-in)
  double-sided white satin ribbon
1 metre (1⅛ yards) 12-mm (½-in)
  white satin ribbon
rose petal cutters
rose calyx cutters
rose leaf cutters, small, medium and large
jasmine cutter
large blossom cutter
plastic leaf veiner
gum arabic

Number of portions
50

Amount of work involved
Approximately 10 hours

Single-tier petal-shaped cakes are very popular because they offer scope for so many different types of decoration. Here, most of the classic sugarpaste techniques are used — the delicate double frill, the flowing embroidery and the use of a large spray of sugar roses and stephanotis with rose buds, leaves and green and white ribbon loops. Because much of the surface of the cake is left undecorated, the sugarpaste must be applied extremely carefully and smoothly over the base layer of marzipan, but before applying it set 225g (8oz) aside. Pay particular attention to the concave sections where the petals meet, if necessary erasing any marks by rubbing them away with the fleshy part of your thumb or the base of your palm. The friction and warmth of your hand will be enough to make the surface smooth again. Leave the cake for at least 24 hours, if not longer, until the sugarpaste has hardened considerably.

Position the cake on the board. Make a template of the embroidery from the pattern provided, then scribe it on to the cake — the pattern is used three times around the sides of the cake. Using a No1 nozzle and plain white royal icing of a piping consistency, pipe a beaded border around the base of the cake. Pipe over the scribed outlines with a No0 nozzle and white royal icing of a piping consistency. On the parts of the design where the icing pattern broadens out to represent garlands or ribbons, increase the pressure on the piping bag and use a fine paintbrush to smooth and shape the icing.

The two rows of frills *(see page 52)* are made from the remaining sugarpaste, which can be mixed with up to 125g (4oz) pastillage to give a firmer finish. To make the lower frill, colour half the sugarpaste with equal amounts of moss green and apple green food colourings until you achieve a deep and even colour. When positioning the frills, leave about 6-mm (¼-in) between the lower green one and the upper white one. There are several ways to disguise the join where the frill meets the cake, and here the rounded end of a No1 dogbone modelling tool has been used to press the top edge of the frill into the sugarpaste. If the cake covering is still fresh and soft, you can use crimpers, such as the No2 scallop or the No6 vee, to make the distinctive line at the join. This creates an effect similar to stitches on a piece of needlepoint.

The large triangular spray of flowers, leaves and ribbons is attached to the top of the cake with a block of sugarpaste.

If you wish to decorate the cake board so it blends in with your design, choose a strong paper that will remain stable when moistened with glue — metallised gift wrapping paper is often the best choice. Avoid cheap uncoated papers or those which have been printed with very heavy layers of ink as they could contaminate the cake. Mark around the outline of the cake board on the wrong side of the paper, then draw another line 5-cm (2-in) outside it. Cut around this line, then make a series of scissor cuts about 2.5-cm (1-in) apart from the edge to the inside line. Spray adhesive on to the top of the board, then place it in the centre of the cut sheet of paper and smooth into place. Spray adhesive to the cut edges of paper, then fold each one in turn over the side and on to the back of the board. If you wish to cover the back of the board, make this piece slightly smaller than the board itself, but still large enough to hide the cut edges of the pieces of paper and to give a neat finish. Then cover the edge of the board with a piece of ribbon or banding that has been sprayed with adhesive.

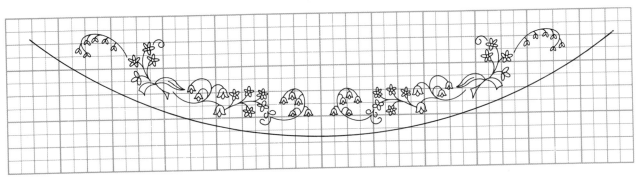

Captivating cascades

The most important ingredient in the successful completion of this cake is time. To decorate a cake to this standard you must allow yourself about two weeks if you are proposing to work on it for two to three hours a day, or at least three full days if you concentrate for long periods without a break.

Cover the cakes with a layer of marzipan and one of sugarpaste in the usual way, and leave to dry. Using a No0 or No1 nozzle and white royal icing of a piping consistency, pipe a line of beading around the bottom edge of each cake. Make a template of the embroidery design for each tier (see page 78). Scribe the outlines on to the sides of the cakes, then pipe on the embroidery using white royal icing of a piping consistency. Use a No0 nozzle for the flowers and stylised V-shaped leaves, and a No00 nozzle for the dots between the groups of flowers. Complete the remaining designs with pink-coloured icing and a No00 nozzle.

Scribe the scallop pattern, over which the lace will be placed, on the top surface of all three tiers and overpipe the scribed line with a small scallop shape, using a No0 nozzle and white royal icing. The embroidery pattern, which is placed in the centre of the middle and lower tiers, is also piped with a No0 nozzle and white royal icing. Next, mark the positions of the cake pillars, noting that three, and not four, pillars are used for each cake and that on the lower tier they are located on a line running from the apex of the extension work to the centre of the middle cake. Set the flowers in position by sticking a sausage of sugarpaste into each of the areas where they will be placed, and using it as a pin cushion for the wired ends of the flowers, sprays, stamens and ribbons. Attach the unwired briar roses with a dab of royal icing.

Before piping any of the bridgework, apply a light dusting of pink powder colour to the roughly triangular area of icing that will lie beneath the curtain of extension work. Using pink-coloured royal icing and a No1 nozzle, pipe the first of the lower lines of bridgework from one side of the triangle to the other. Leave to dry for a few minutes, then pipe another line against the first, but slightly shorter at each end. Leave to dry and then repeat the process, each time making the line slightly shorter until you have built out five lines, then pipe the last two rows right from the start of the triangle to the end, so that when the bridge-work is completed there are seven rows of icing joined horizontally. If a strand of icing does not cling to its neighbour, it can be gently coaxed into position with the moistened tip of a fine sable paintbrush.

Pipe the first row of bridgework in pink for the upper extension and then pipe the lower row of the extension using white royal icing and a No00 nozzle. It may help to place the cake on a tilting turntable so that when the cake is tilted towards you, the icing strands of the extension fall vertically and do not sag as they dry. Pipe each line very carefully, starting just under the first row of upper bridgework. It is most important to maintain a uniform distance between each strand and to ensure that they are all vertical and not leaning to the left or right. Take the tip of the nozzle past the bridgework and then use a damp brush to smooth away the lower end of the strands below where they join the bridgework. When the lower level of extension work is completed, revert to the pink-coloured icing and a No1 nozzle and continue to pipe the bridgework for the upper level. Use the same procedure as before, but be careful not to accidentally break any of the work already completed. Pipe the vertical strings of the extension as before with white icing and a No00 nozzle.

Only when this part of the decoration has been completed should the lacework be placed in position. Use a very small amount of royal icing to pipe tiny 12-mm (½-in) lines alongside and under-neath the piped scallop line and lift the lace from its backing paper on the blade of a palette knife. Pick each piece up with your fingers and gently place it in position, at a slight angle so that it leans towards the sides of the cake, on the piped line of icing, adjusting it with the soft hairs of a fine sable paintbrush. Lacework is also applied in a graceful curve to the areas above the extension work, with the lace at the apex of the triangle standing out from the cake at right angles and each subsequent piece leaning downwards at a slightly increasing angle, so that the lowest pieces on either side are set at about 45° to the sugarpaste.

The top piece consists of flowers set in a two-piece pastillage vase made in a plastic mould (see page 34). Each section is shaped like a deeply fluted fairy cake pan, 3.75-cm (1½-in) wide and with a flat base. When each part is hard, turn one upside down. Place the other half on top of it and fix in place with royal icing. Fill the shallow bowl of the vase with sugarpaste and set the flowers in it, so they trail in a natural manner over the edge.

Possible piping problems
There are only two troublesome problems associated with extension work, both of which can be easily overcome. Firstly, if the icing thread keeps breaking, this is because an even pressure is not being maintained on the piping bag, or because the icing is too soft. Secondly, if the icing is expelled in a curling or spiralling motion, this is either because the point of the tube is damaged or because there may be a particle of sugar lodged in the top of the nozzle. Alternatively, you may not be keeping an even pressure on the piping bag or moving the nozzle at the same rate at which the icing is being squeezed through it.

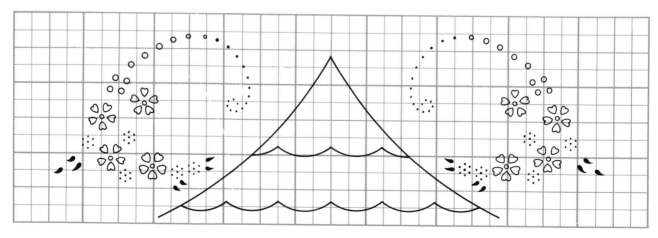

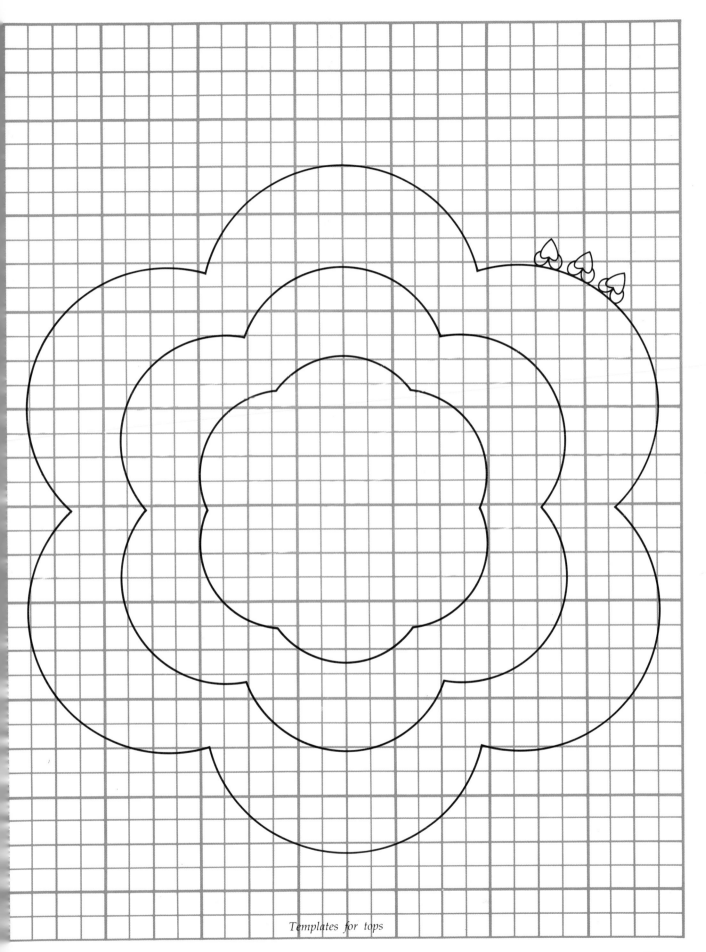

Templates for tops

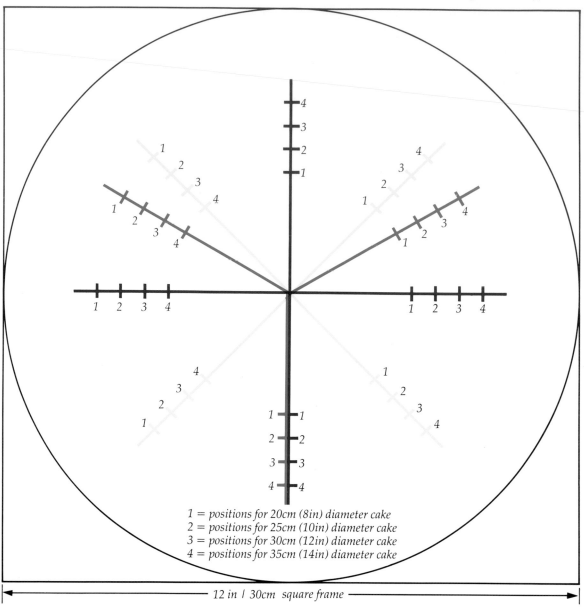

4
3
2
1

1 2 3 4   1 2 3 4

1 = positions for 20cm (8in) diameter cake
2 = positions for 25cm (10in) diameter cake
3 = positions for 30cm (12in) diameter cake
4 = positions for 35cm (14in) diameter cake

1 1
2 2
3 3
4 4

12 in / 30cm square frame

For round tiered cakes, follow positions marked on the red lines.

For square tiered cakes, follow positions marked on the yellow lines.

For heart–, hexagonal- and petal-shaped cakes, follow positions marked on the blue lines.

Centre a full-size template on the bottom tier. Mark the relevant positions on the icing by pricking through the tracing paper with a scriber. Repeat the procedure for the remaining tiers. It is not necessary to enclose the template in a square or circle.